The Lord's Prayer

Martin Chemnitz

Translated by Georg Williams

SAINT LOUIS

*To my daughter Rachel
and all other lambs of God
who by their Baptism may say
"Our Father."*

All Scripture quotations, unless otherwise indicated, are taken from the HOLY BIBLE, NEW INTERNATIONAL VERSION®. NIV®. Copyright © 1973, 1978, 1984 by International Bible Society. Used by permission of Zondervan Publishing House. All rights reserved.

Copyright © 1999 Concordia Publishing House
3558 S. Jefferson Avenue, St. Louis, MO 63118-3968
Manufactured in the United States of America

All rights reserved. No part of this publication may be reproduced, stored in a retrieval system, or transmitted, in any form or by any means, electronic, mechanical, photocopying, recording, or otherwise, without the prior written permission of Concordia Publishing House.

Library of Congress Cataloging-in-Publication Data

Chemnitz, Martin, 1522–1586.

    The Lord's Prayer/Martin Chemnitz; translated by [i.e. edited by] Georg Williams.
      p. cm.
    Includes bibliographical references and index.
    ISBN 0-570-04283-6
     1. Lord's Prayer—Early works to 1800. I. Williams, Georg. II. Title.
    BV230 C26 2000
    226.9'606—dc21

                                          99-053101

1 2 3 4 5 6 7 8 9 10   08 07 06 05 04 03 02 01 00 99

CONTENTS

The Man, the Theologian, the Pastor

INTRODUCTION TO THE NEW EDITION

he Lutheran Reformation would have fallen into decay and eventually failed had it not been for the second Martin, Martin Chemnitz. "If Martin [Chemnitz] had not come, Martin [Luther] would hardly have stood."[1] This bold statement was not made by a devotee of Chemnitz or even by one of his fellow Lutherans. This summary of the impact Chemnitz exerted on the Reformation was made by a Roman Catholic theologian against whom Chemnitz had so forcibly argued. After Luther's death, the Lutheran movement drifted into such theological and political diversity that this disarray eventually would have led to its fragmentation and demise. Chemnitz stepped into this arena with his deliberate, systematic, and pastoral method and became a major force in the unification that was achieved in the Formula of Concord. Without his efforts, much of the Lutheran realm would have fallen into such confusion that soon Roman tradition would have again dominated European Christianity.

"Of the great sixteenth-century theologians ... Chemnitz was the greatest."[2] Born on November 9, 1522, he spent his entire life in the pursuit of knowledge; after studying in several places, he received his master's degree in 1548 from the University of Koenigsberg. His endeavors in life were learning, teaching, and preaching. He thoroughly studied the church fathers during his tenure as Ducal Librarian in Koenigsberg. During this time he was able to amass an amazing, even profound, knowledge of the history and doctrines of

---

1. Martin Chemnitz, *The Two Natures in Christ*, trans. J. A. O. Preus (St. Louis: Concordia, 1971), p. 9

2. *Ibid.*, p. 9

the church. Quotations from the church fathers are used in almost all of his writings as he demonstrated the antiquity of the Lutheran movement. As Luther taught, this movement was not to form a new church but to reform it and return it to the one true Church.

Chemnitz was also a penetrating biblical theologian. His systematic mind was sharpened by the many challenging books of the Ducal Library. With this well-stocked library at his fingertips, he created a plan for the proper use of such wealth which, in turn, demonstrated his devotion to the Bible. The editions of Old and New Testaments were the first he studied. Then and only then could he study the commentaries on the Scriptures. After exhausting the exegetical material in the Koenigsberg Ducal Library, Chemnitz studied the church fathers, beginning with their most ancient works. He was truly a methodical and precise theologian. His works, especially the *Examen* and *De Duabus*, beautifully show his precision. With the precision of his theology and his grasp of the ancient church fathers, Chemnitz wielded a sharp two-edged sword that he used for the unification of the Lutheran movement. Joined by such men as Selnecker, Chytreas, and Andreae, Martin Chemnitz was a main contributor to the Formula of Concord. Although he was successful in other regions, Chemnitz was neither able to get his own duke, the Duke of Braunschweig, nor his duchy to append their names to the *Concordia*.

But for Chemnitz, theology existed to serve the church. Everything a theologian did had to be pastoral; it had to serve the good of the people for whom he cared. Chemnitz was never a university professor, as Luther and Melanchthon had been. Ordained in the church at Braunschweig in 1547, he began his lifelong task of being a parish pastor. He saw his vocation only in the context of his constant association with the common people of the church. He knew that theological exercises were of no avail unless they affected the lives and spirituality of the children of God. He remained, however, a capable academic theologian, taking his doctorate from the University of Rostock in 1568.

Chemnitz was a simple man, a gentle shepherd of God's little lambs. He was reared neither in the scarcity of a monastery nor the comfort of a wealthy home. He lost his father when he was very young, so his older brother cared for the family by continuing the family business as a merchant trading in wool. The large family led a life that was neither secure nor conducive to costly education. Only through the influence of a local businessman was Chemnitz able to be formally educated. His family situation was not so unlike that of the first Martin; and like Luther, he wrote for the instruction of the common people of God: a catechism, hymns, devotional sermons, and the like. One gets a glimpse of this gentle pastor in his sermons, which were doctrinal, short, simple, and clear.

Martin Chemnitz experienced several unsettling incidents when he associated with the nobility, yet his manner of presenting the Gospel of the Lord Jesus Christ always brought him back into good favor with his princes and lords. The glorious message of the newly begun reformation of the Christian church was at the heart and center of all his work. The theological emphasis of the fathers of the Lutheran movement found expression in the pastoral qualities of the man who was the "noble conservator of the theological treasures of the Reformation."[3]

---

3. *Ibid.*, p. 9

His Book on Prayer

A Substantial and Godly Exposition of the Prayer Commonly Called the Lord's Prayer is one of sixty-five of Chemnitz' works. The Latin original of this work on the Lord's Prayer does not exist. The first known English copy, published in 1598 by Mr. John Legate, the printer at the University of Cambridge, raises an interesting question: Why was this work by Chemnitz translated into English at such an early date?

I contacted the University of Cambridge in England and found that they did have a copy of the original English translation of this work at one time. They believed that they were the only source of such a copy. However, the actual volume was not to be found; they presumed that it had been lost during World War II. The existent photocopy is of a type style and printing practice that would date the publication to the time of Mr. John Legate.

The printer appends an introduction in which he leaves as anonymous the translator of the work from Latin into English. At that time in England, theological works were extremely popular, especially those of Martin Luther, and the press was considered powerful. Printing was permitted only in London, Oxford, and Cambridge, and even then only under extreme supervision. John Legate was the authorized printer at the University of Cambridge. It was a time of renegade presses when Catholics and Puritan extremists voiced explosive opinions. Elizabeth I wanted to end this practice of unauthorized publishing, permitting only proper books to be printed and sold. Yet book-selling was a very lucrative venture, and books were often surreptitiously printed in England or smuggled into the country from the European mainland. If Chemnitz' *Lord's Prayer* were printed at Cambridge as titled, it would have undergone extensive examination.

Although England was experiencing religious unrest and change, nothing in the content of this work suggests an effect on the outcome of any movement of the day. No propaganda reason seems to exist for the appearance of this work other than the desire for an excellent devotional booklet on the Lord's Prayer. Its printing would have ranged from 100–500 copies. Since no original copies exist, it is assumed that the work, though profitable in content, failed monetarily and was limited to a very short printing. The work has possibly been lost to the world in its original form, but photocopies of the English translation do exist now in various places.

The Task of This Edition

The compilation of this new edition has an interesting history. In the 1982 master's thesis I wrote for Concordia Theological Seminary, Fort Wayne, my goal was to change as little as possible from the 1598 English edition. I felt that one level of possible change and mistranslation had already occurred. To make changes from the 1598 English edition would compound not only the number of potential mistranslations, but also possibly increase the errors of the mistranslations, if any, of the 1598 English edition.

My 1982 master's thesis attempted to make the stilted and antiquated language usable by the theological audience, not necessarily the common reader. This new volume will leave the safety of little change and attempt to make Chemnitz' work on the Lord's Prayer available in a readable fashion for the common twentieth-century American reader.

One must understand that for any research of Chemnitz' *Lord's Prayer* to be truly theological, it must return to at least the 1982 master's thesis,[4] if not to the 1598 edition. Even if this were done, a question-instilling gap may still be caused by the lack of the original Latin edition.

---

4. Georg Williams, "A New Edition of Martin Chemnitz' *'A Substantial and Godly Exposition of the Prayer Commonly Called the Lord's Prayer'* " (master's thesis, Concordia Theological Seminary, Fort Wayne, Indiana, 1982).

THE PRINTER
OF THE 1598
EDITION,
MR. JOHN
LEGATE,
TO THE
READER

hristian reader, although the very name of the author of this exposition sufficiently commends this work to you, yet because I have undertaken publishing it even though so many labors of our own learned and godly countrymen have faithfully written on the Lord's Prayer, I thought it not wrong in a word or two to give some reason for my work. First of all, the excellence of this exposition, which I commend not so much of my own knowledge but upon the judgment of very godly and learned men, moved me to publish it for the whole country. The praise which seems peculiar to it comes from a double fountain: first, from the learned interpretation of the words in their native sense; second, from the ample and plain explanation of the true and complete meaning of the Spirit of God in every petition. In this, Chemnitz has endeavored to set down the true and complete interpretation of the words in the Greek and Hebrew tongues, showing what blessings we are to ask and what sins we must bewail. He has done this not only that the simple, by the blessing of God upon their endeavor, may in short time learn to pray in faith and in obedience, but also that the godly and the learned who have attained to a higher level of knowledge and grace may increase their knowledge and further edify themselves in their most holy faith. Thus desiring for you to have the spirit of prayer which may teach you to use this means so that you may pray with the Spirit and also with understanding, I take my leave and here end.

Chapter 1

AN INTRODUCTION

The necessity and benefit of using prayer troubles not only the trivial objections of profane persons but also the conceit in the hearts of the godly themselves. Firstly, if God knows what we want before we ask it, what need is there or what good does it do to ask our desires of him who knows them already? Such prayers are likely to bother and grieve, say these people. Jerome finely replies, "In prayer we are not showers, but suitors." It is one thing to make known to him who is ignorant and another thing to beg and ask of him who already knows. Even this answer does not remove all difficulty. For our heavenly Father not only knows what things we want, but also, unasked of his fatherly care and favor, he is ready and active to help us of his own will even before we ask. Therefore, it seems, there is neither benefit in nor need of praying.

I answer that we do not pray with that intent. We, by our prayers, cannot stir up God and put him in mind of his duty. We do not pray to show he is negligent and careless of our affairs. We do not view God as being hard and merciless or try to allure him by our prayers in order to change his mind. We know indeed that he is ready, of his own will, to give good things, especially to those who repent and humble themselves under the mighty hand of God—those who by faith do seek, knock, and ask. Therefore, we do pour out our prayers before God, not because we doubt his good will, but rather that in faith we may pray with true repentance. He has promised forgiveness of sins to those who repent (Ezek. 18:23). He will lessen his judgments and bestow his blessings (Jer. 18:8). He will give grace to the humble (1 Pet. 5:5). When we call upon God and think upon his promises, we bring with us and likewise exercise true faith. We do this because the Lord has promised all good things to him who knocks and asks (Matt. 7:7). We also "approach the throne of grace with confidence, so that we may receive mercy and find grace to help in our time of need" (Heb. 4:16). Likewise, spiritual blessings cannot be received by any other means than faith. Indeed, bodily or outward benefits are often bestowed upon the wicked as well. But, so that these benefits may be profitable for us, it is the will of God that we should wait for them in hope and receive them by faith from his fatherly hand. Therefore, we pray in faith that we may desire to receive from God not only corporal blessings, but especially those blessings that are spiritual, heavenly, and eternal.

We also pray in faith that we would receive from God the blessings of this life and that by his blessings they may be profitable for us. Because God would have this glory given to himself as the Fountain, Author, and Giver of every good thing (James 1:17) and that we should wholly rely upon him, therefore we, in prayer, testify that we neither ascribe them to any other nor seek them elsewhere. We completely hope for, expect, and require the same from God alone. For God has promised that he will be ready and willing to help. In our prayers we lay our wants and needs before God, not as though he[1] did not know them, but that by pouring out our cares into the Lord's bosom, we may unburden and comfort our souls. This promise is very sweet and comforting (Ps. 37:5; 55:22). "Cast all your anxiety on him because he cares for you" (1 Pet. 5:7). Chrysostom adds this reason why we should pray: "That by often calling upon God we may become familiar with him."[2] He urges prayer that we may more highly esteem and more reverently use that which God bestows upon us when we ask and knock.

We should carefully think on the necessity and benefit of prayer, lest we become too cold and too slow in prayer because conceitedly we think that God is ready to help us of his own accord. We will then allow ourselves to stop the exercise of prayer. We should not abuse the most sweet sentence of the ready and good will of God toward us. It should rather be an inducement and a motive to cause and confirm our diligence and confidence in prayer. There are some who think or at least trouble themselves with these conceits: that unasked, before we pray, God not only knows what he will do and what he will give but even beforehand has set it down and appointed it.

Therefore, we either ask in vain that which otherwise will not happen or else we wickedly pray, as though we hoped by our prayer to turn God from his firm decree and purpose and make him changeable and non-constant. To this objection some answer: if that which we ask is ordained by God, then we pray upon good and sure confidence; if it is not, we do not hinder or stop God's predestination because we pray God's will be done. Luther's exposition is more plain and safe. His explanation is that we are not commanded to busy ourselves about the hidden foreknowledge of God or to search into his secret counsels, but rather we must dispose ourselves accord-

1. The 1598 text has "we."

2. Unknown reference.

15

ing to his will revealed to us in his Word. There he teaches that by repentance and by prayer God's wrath is appeased, many dangers and evils avoided, and many benefits obtained (Jer. 18:8, Ezek. 33:11, 1 Kings 8:56). Therefore, he has commanded us to pray. In fact, he is angry when a man does not come before the Lord in prayer, specifically so that his land may not be destroyed (Ezek. 22:30).

Two reasons, therefore, warn us to pray: 1) God of his own will is ready to help and knows what we want and what he himself will do, and 2) it is his will and command that we should pray. While thinking on the secret foreknowledge of God, we must not come up with or allow some exceptions to those things that are plainly revealed and commanded in the Word. If you cannot reconcile them, leave that to the hidden reasons of God's secret foreknowledge. Concerning those things that are commanded and appointed in the revealed Word about prayer, this is what you are to do, that is, you are to pray and pray continually. I have noted these things by reminding you of that saying, "Your Father knows what you need before you ask him" (Matt. 6:8).

Our Savior Christ, when giving this prayer, begins with this commandment: "This, then, is how you should pray" (Matt. 6:9). He would not bind those whom he teaches to pray with this set number of words codifying a good work, for that would make prayer to be babble indeed. The apostles themselves, in their acts and epistles, often prayed using other words even after the delivery and receiving of this form from our Savior Christ. The strongest proof is that Matthew and Luke, in recording this Lord's Prayer, curiously do not record it in the same words. Our Savior Christ showed his disciples the way to pray in a short example. His custom was to teach a general doctrine by giving a particular example in which we may understand the general doctrine.

Therefore, in this pattern of prayer his purpose is to show the following: 1) how small a number of words we can use in prayer, contrary to the vain babbling of the Pharisees and of the heathen; 2) upon whom is to be called or to whom we must direct our prayers; 3) with what confidence we must pray; 4) how and for what reasons; 5) what things we are to ask; 6) in what order; 7) by what means; and 8) for what end. All the principal points, which are required in true prayer, are thus contained in this pattern. Augustine, in his *Epistle to Proba*, both truly and finely said, "We have liberty in prayer to use other words just that we say the same things which this prayer contains. We do not have liberty to say other, differing, or contrary things."[3] Similarly Matthew says, "This, then, is how you should pray" (6:9). The saying of Christ, "When you pray, say…" (Luke 11:2), is in agreement. Here Augustine puts forward this question: "If we must not use many words in prayer because our heavenly Father knows our wants, by the same reason and for the same cause, we should not use few words, no, not even those words which are here appointed by our Savior Christ."[4]

The answer is that, in regard to God and by his doing, we need neither many, nor few, nor any words at all in prayer; neither does the form of prayer consist in the repetition of words. For to pray is to lift up the mind to God, to pour out the heart before God, and to ask something of him. No man truly asks for anything if he does not want it. Desire is an affectation of the mind. Therefore, though he utters with the mouth the best words that can be uttered, unless his mind with attention and devotion asks for it also and the heart truly desires that for which he asks, that man simply does not pray.

But he that lifts up his mind and with a devout inward affection of heart entirely asks anything of God, that man truly prays although he may not express his desire in words. One man cannot ask another unless he uses words or gestures. But the inward and the most secret corners of the mind

3. Augustine, "Letter to Proba," *The Writings of St. Augustine*, trans. Sister Wilfred Parsons, S. N. D., II (New York: Fathers of the Church, 1953), p. 394.

4. *Ibid*.

and heart are plainly seen by God. David says, "My sighing is not hidden from you" (Ps. 38:9). "You hear, O LORD, the desire of the afflicted; you encourage them, and you listen to their cry" (Ps. 10:17). And again, in Psalm 38:9 he says, "All my longings lie open before you." "We do not know what we ought to pray for, but the Spirit himself intercedes for us with groans that words cannot express" (Rom. 8:26).

It would be a foolish thing, therefore, to utter our prayer in words as though God could not understand the desires of our hearts. Yet the saints of God in the Old Testament and the apostles in the New Testament used words in praying. With reason Christ says in Luke's Gospel, "When you pray, say…" (11:2). Was it not for our sakes and for our prayers? We should carefully consider this so that we may learn to use vocal prayer properly and profitably. Our mind does not thoroughly consider or regard those things that we want or those things for which we ask. This is especially true if they are spiritual or pertain to the glory of God. Therefore, the words we use in praying are an advertisement that directs us to consider those things so that the desire of our heart may be rightly directed.

In prayer the heart ought to be penitent and humble. But because we for the most part rush into prayer without proper consideration of our sins and unworthiness, the practiced use of words is profitable. For if the mind gives heed, "I will sing with my spirit, but I will also sing with my mind" (1 Cor. 14:15). Thus this meditation prepares the heart for serious repentance and true humility. The desires of our hearts are commonly so out of order that men neither think about the order nor the outcome of those things that they request. But the words we use in prayer make us aware of those things upon which we are to think when we pray. Doubtless the rehearsing of and meditating on God's promises stir up, kindle, and increase our faith. We are often slow to pray and pray when we are cold and drowsy. We do not come to God with the devotion of mind with which we ought to come. But when praying we repeat words, with diligent meditation and proper thought on the promise and commandment, and our mind directs itself to God. Our devotion is kindled, and once being kindled it is continued and increased. By the words of our prayer, we are put in mind of those things for which we are to ask. This diligent meditation excites and kindles our numb and frozen heart to a love of prayer. For those words, because they are the words of Christ, are the tool and instrument of the Spirit, whereby the spirit of prayer will be powerful and effectual in us all. Therefore, the words that Christ delivers, "When you pray, say…," bid us to push forward. The rehearsal of words in prayer is used to excite and kindle, to continue and increase our devotion, lest it should wax cold, be numbed, and be extinguished altogether.

Sometimes longer prayers serve best; sometimes those which are shorter are best. For this reason Augustine in his one hundred and twenty-first *Epistle to Proba* thoroughly writes many things, some that pertain to this topic. These I will set down.

> He who forbids much babbling in prayer because he knows what is needful for us does likewise command that we should always pray and not faint. We should do this not because he would have our will made known to him, whereof he cannot be ignorant, but to exercise our desire whereby we may receive that which we are about to ask. That which he would give is very great, but we are little and shortsighted and cannot receive the same. Therefore, it is said unto us, 'open your mouth'; for so much the more fully shall we receive that which is exceedingly great by how much we do more faithfully believe it, more firmly hope for it, and more earnestly desire it.[5]

---

5. *Ibid.*, p. 398.

Therefore, we always desire to pray in faith, hope, and charity. Yet at certain times we pray to the Lord with words so that we may remind ourselves how much we have benefited by praying and urge ourselves to cheerfully pray more. Therefore, when the apostle says, "Pray continually" (1 Thess. 5:17), it is nothing else than this: continually desire a blessed life. Therefore at certain hours we withdraw our mind from other cares and business. Through this our desire to pray is increased. Through this we urge ourselves to give heed to that which we desire. We do this so that our desire to pray is not waxed cold and eventually put out. Therefore we constantly urge ourselves to pray more often. To pray a long time is not, as some think, to babble. The use of many words is one thing; long-continued affection is another thing. It is said of the Lord himself that he continued whole nights in prayer and used to pray a very long time. The brethren in Egypt are said to pray very often yet very briefly. In this way they pray quickly lest by praying longer the earnestness that was carefully begun should become dull and disappear. By this they sufficiently declare that this earnestness, just as it is not to be forced when it is not there, is not quickly to be stopped if it wants to go on longer. For in prayer we must use many words and yet we must not go on if our earnestness fades.

To pray much is to knock at the door of him to whom we pray with a continual and a godly attention of the heart. For the most part, this business is better performed in sighs and groans than with words—better by weeping than by speaking. Our groaning is not hidden from him who by his Word made all things and desires, not the words of man. But we must use words in prayer so that we may be reminded to be respectful for what we ask. We also are not to think that we teach or move the Lord. Augustine teaches these same things. For this reason Paul appoints the public reciting of prayers and psalms in the Church. "Let the word of Christ dwell in you richly as you teach and admonish one another with all wisdom, and as you sing psalms, hymns and spiritual songs with gratitude in your hearts to God" (Col. 3:16). "When you come together, everyone has a hymn, or a word of instruction, a revelation, a tongue or an interpretation. All of these must be done for the strengthening of the church" (1 Cor. 14:26). Because it is sometimes needful to use words in prayer, there can be no prayer more profitable than that which the Lord himself delivered and appointed. For first of all, it briefly comprehends all those things that can be properly and profitably asked of the Lord. It shows of whom we must ask them, in what manner and order, and for what end and purpose. Augustine says, "If you shall peruse the words of the prayers of all the saints of God which are extant in the whole Scripture and chiefly in the Psalms, you will find nothing which is not briefly contained and concluded in this Lord's Prayer."[6]

Second, as the Creed is the rule of faith, so the Lord's Prayer is the rule of all prayers. For he who desires anything in prayer, says Augustine, or speaks anything that cannot pertain to the evangelical prayer, can be assured that his prayer is not spiritual but carnal and unlawful.[7]

Third, as for authority, the Son of God himself, who is our Advocate, who brings our prayers to the Father, who obtains for us the spirit of prayer, who together with the Father hears us, prescribed for us this pattern of prayer. It is a friendly and familial prayer, says Cyprian, to entreat the Father by the words of the Son. The Father will acknowledge the words of the Son when we pray. Then we have Christ our Advocate speaking with the Father for our sins. Let us propound the words of our Advocate when we miserable sinners beg forgiveness for our sins. Cyprian says these things.[8]

It is only rashness and impiety that disdains either the shortness or the simplicity of the Lord's Prayer as though you

---

6. Augustine, "Letters to Proba," p. 394.

7. *Ibid.*, p. 393.

8. Cyprian, "On the Lord's Prayer," Treatise IV, paragraph 3.

yourself could find or compose a better pattern of prayer. Yet the recitation of the Lord's Prayer must not be vain mumbling, as though the words uttered without understanding had some magical force. We must consider what the words signify. We must remind ourselves of how far they reach and how many things they contain so that we may pray with the spirit and with the mind (1 Cor. 14:15). In these petitions we include our wants. By these means, as it has been said, these words will arouse our devotion. Let us therefore briefly consider every point and compare the text of Matthew with that which is set down by Luke. For although, according to Luke, Christ repeated this pattern of prayer at another time and situation than the one Matthew records, yet because the pattern is the same in both places, the comparison will be profitable.

Here we must observe that some Latin books, omitting some things, record this form of prayer more briefly in Luke than it is recorded by Matthew. For in the beginning it says only, "Father." "Who art in heaven" follows in Matthew, but in Luke this phrase is omitted. The third petition, "Your will be done in earth as it is in heaven," also is omitted in Luke. "But deliver us from evil" is omitted as well. Augustine says expressly in his *Enchiridion*,[9] chapters 115 and 116, that the Lord's Prayer in Matthew contains seven petitions, but in Luke it has not seven but only five petitions. He shows that the petition "Your will be done" is contained in the two previous petitions. The petition "Deliver us from evil" is also contained in that which went before, namely, "Lead us not into temptation." From this I gather that the Latin books, even in Augustine's time, had the Lord's Prayer in Luke as it is now read. The Greek books set down the whole prayer in Luke as it is in Matthew, except that Luke concludes "for yours is the kingdom." One might think that the petitions

---

9. Augustine, *The Enchiridion of Faith, Hope, and Love*, trans. J. F. Shaw (Chicago: Henry Regenery, 1961), p. 132.

missing in Luke have been added from the Greek books of Matthew. But Augustine in his book, *Of the Words of the Lord*, commenting on Luke chapter 28, and Ambrose in his first book of the Sacrament,[10] chapter 4, records the whole prayer out of Luke as it is in Matthew. From this I gather that the Latin books differed at that time. Some editions read it in Luke as it is in the Greek, while others read it as it is in the common Latin. As for the differences in some words, we will address them in the exposition in each place. But that very diversity of words shows that we are not bound to a superstitious recitation of words in prayer.

This prayer contains three parts: the entrance or preface, the petitions, and the conclusion, each of which I will speak in order.

---

10. Ambrose, "The Fifth Book of the Sacraments," *Patrologiae Cursus Completus Patrologiae Latinae*, accurante J. P. Migne, XVI (Paris: Apud Garnier Fratres, 1880), p. 469. The original text has "The First Book of the Sacraments," but it should be "The Fifth Book of the Sacraments."

Chapter 2

"OUR FATHER" – THE PREFACE

Augustine says that in every earnest request we ought to obtain the good will of whom we make our request. This is most easily done by reciting the praise and commendation of the greatness of the one to whom we pray. Therefore, seeing that we neither can nor ought to boast of our own merits before God, in the beginning of this prayer Christ has commanded us to say nothing else but "our Father." Hugo says that Christ, like a good orator, before the petitions, prefixes a short preface. In it grace is requested from the person asked when we say "Father" and for the person asking when we say "our."[1] Surely these thoughts have their use. Earlier we stated that we should not use words in prayer to move the mind of God by rhetorical manipulation. But rather than reciting and meditating on the words, we use them to move ourselves to attention, devotion, confidence, and care to frame our prayers properly. Through this we show ourselves to be suitors the Lord would have. Therefore, those words are

---

1. Hugo, *Patrologiae Cursus Completus Patrologiae Latinae*, accurante J. P. Migne, CLXXV (Paris: Apud Garnier Fratres, 1879), p. 768.

principally to be employed for this end and purpose. We will briefly explain in several points those things that are principally to be thought upon by the occasion of these words.

First, the words "our Father" cause us to understand that prayer ought not to be approached in a wishing manner. For example, some men like to say "Please God, let this good thing happen to me," "Oh, take away this danger or this evil," "God bless it and prosper it," "God forbid," and others like this. But we must expressly name him not in general terms only, as when we say "God grant; God forbid," but we must expressly name him when we speak unto and call upon him that our prayer may be directed unto him, "our Father," as if it were communication. Since the Psalms speak in the third person, as in "God be merciful unto us; God bless us," we must understand prayer is to be directed either through the Mediator or to the second person. When directing it through the Mediator we ask that for his sake God would be merciful unto us and bless us. Sometimes the devotion of the mind is to be referred to the second person. The usual phrase of Scripture is to speak unto a person present using the third person, as in "Let my lord go on ahead of his servant" (Gen. 33:14), "Let our lord command…" (1 Sam. 16:16), and "May my lord pay no attention to that wicked man Nabal" (1 Sam. 25:25). The usual phrase of Scripture, "Let my lord live," is to be understood as "I pray God that my lord may live." Therefore, in whatsoever words the prayer is framed, the mind must always think upon God and behold him. This is done so that our desires and requests may be directed unto him. This is the norm and rule of our prayer, to say, "our Father."

Second, these words urge us to remember that prayer or invocation is not to be directed to any creature but only to the heavenly Father. We may not direct our prayers to those whose spirits we are sure live with God, for the name "Father" is also opposed to even these. "But you are our Father, though Abraham does not know us or Israel acknowledge us; you, Oh LORD, are our Father, our Redeemer from of old is your name" (Is. 63:16).

Third, the words "our Father" teach us that we must think of God and speak to God in prayer as he has revealed his essence to us in his Word. When the heathen go to pray, they think of a god who is eternal, almighty, and the creator, but they do not know who that god is. We are taught by these words to make a difference between our calling upon God and the prayers of the heathen. We are to think that we call upon God who has made known his being unto us in his Word, that he is the Father, the Son, and the Holy Ghost. He is the Father of our Lord Jesus Christ who sends the Spirit of his Son into the hearts of the faithful, whereby we cry, "Abba, Father." So the word "Father" is to be understood essentially in this place for God, that is, the Divine Majesty, the whole Trinity, Father, Son, and Holy Ghost. As it is written, "Is he not your Father, your Creator, who made you and formed you?" (Deut. 32:6). "But you are our Father, though Abraham does not know us or Israel acknowledge us; you, Oh LORD, are our Father, our Redeemer from of old is your name" (Is. 63:16). The Son also is called by this general title, Father of Eternity (Is. 9:6). The Holy Ghost is called the Father of the poor.

This title therefore teaches us to set our mind against all flippancy, inconsiderateness, and pride when we are about to pray. In such devotion, reverence, and humility we are to remember that we pour out the words of our prayer, not into the air or before any creatures, but before the Divine Majesty, to whom we come in our prayer. Before the Father we appear (Eph. 3:14) asking him to hear and see all our supplications (Ps. 141:2; Ps. 119:58).

Fourth, the word "Father" also may be properly understood as referring very personally to the Father, the first person of the Divine Majesty. When the Father does something necessarily it includes the Son because the Son is Father. By the Spirit of the Son we cry, "Abba, Father." The distinction of the Trinity in their respective offices and gifts to the church are set forward in our consideration of the preface of this prayer. Thus Paul understood the name "Father" in the prayer in various places and especially in Ephesians 3:14: "For this reason I kneel before the Father." Christ himself explains the words "our Father" when he says in John 20:17, "I am returning to my Father and your Father, to my God and your God."

Therefore, this title "Father" comprises not only the Father from eternity who has begotten his only begotten Son, but in respect of the Father, as the whole Trinity, it contains the benefits of our regeneration, adoption, and calling to a heavenly inheritance. In respect of the Son, the Mediator, it contains the merit, office, and the benefits of his propitiation, reconciliation, and intercession. It urges[2] us to find comfort in that which the Son promises. "My Father will give you whatever you ask in my name" (John 16:23). Because a doubting and distrustful prayer obtains nothing (James 1:6), it is written in Mark 11:24, "Therefore I tell you, whatever you ask for in prayer, believe that you have received it, and it will be yours."

The title "our Father" teaches us with what faith and confidence we are to pray to God. We are not to pray in proud and Pharisaic presumption based on our own justice or worthiness, or on the works or merits either of ourselves or others. We are to pray with the humble acknowledgment and confession of our own unworthiness. We are to pray with the merit and intercession of the only Son of God, our Mediator, through whom the Father has adopted us to be sons and heirs (Eph. 1:5). For Daniel says in his prayer, "Give ear, O God, and hear; open your eyes and see the desolation of the city that bears your Name. We do not make requests of you because we are righteous, but because of your great mercy" (Dan. 9:18).

---

2. The 1598 text has "warns."

Likewise, the fullness of this title "Father" reminds us of a very sweet consolation. We have "a merciful and faithful high priest in service to God" (Heb. 2:17). "But if anybody does sin, we have one who speaks to the Father in our defense.… He is the atoning sacrifice for our sins" (1 John 2:1–2). "He is able to save completely those who come to God through him, because he always lives to intercede for them" (Heb. 7:25, cf. Heb. 9:24). He has received gifts from kings (Ps. 68:29), and he gives the same to us (Eph. 4:11). We are not commanded to call God a lord, just, great, almighty, or terrible, but our Father. By these words those who pray are confident that they will be heard and that they will obtain their requests. "Let us then approach the throne of grace with confidence, so that we may receive mercy and find grace to help us in our time of need" (Heb. 4:16). The saying of Bernard: "That prayer which tastes sweet of a fatherly name gives me assurance that I shall obtain all my requests" is surely sweet. The title "Father" gives us confidence. As Christ himself declares in John 16:23, our prayers are neither grievous nor ungrateful to God. The Father so loves us that he is delighted with this our duty. When we come to him with our prayers, his fatherly mind is full of care for our necessities (Matt. 6:32). Of his own accord he is ready and active to hear and to help us "as a father has compassion on his children" (Ps. 103:13; cf. Lk. 11:9).

Again, this title teaches those who pray to examine themselves, as they are indeed the sons of God, members and brethren of Christ, one engrafted into the Father. For if they go without repenting of their sin and not seeking and embracing Christ by true faith, they cannot call God "Father" unless they believe that by Christ they are reconciled to God. One can see that we are taught many things by this title.

Fifth, whereas we not only say "Father" but "our Father," we are to consider that which Christ says: "I am returning to my Father and your Father, to my God and your God" (John 20:17). Therefore, we should always think that God, who is by nature the Father of Christ, is for his sake by grace also our Father, not by nature but by adoption. Lest we should think that he were only the Father of a few who are endued with great virtues and excellent gifts, when we say "our Father" we include the whole body of believers, even though all the members are not alike. This thought beats down pride and works humility in the children of God who have attained a greater measure of grace. So that they may not consider themselves special in this fatherhood but rather count themselves all alike in the flock of God's children, all say "our Father." This also serves to put courage into the weak so that they may not think themselves to be excluded from this fatherhood. The weak should know that God is no less their Father than the Father of Mary, John the Baptist and Paul. Therefore they are commanded to say "our Father," since we pray to "a Father who judges each man's work impartially" (1 Pet. 1:17).

Finally, this very title urges us to brotherly love; for if there is one who is our Father (Matt. 23:9), then we are all brothers and members of each other. "Have we not all one Father? Did not one God create us? Why do we profane the covenant of our fathers by breaking faith with one another?" (Mal. 2:10). This title also teaches us to pray not only for our own wants but also to pray to God for the necessities of our whole brotherhood and of each member. For we are to say, "our Father: give us, forgive us." We need not doubt if we are members of that body. We realize that the prayers of the whole body also include our needs. For this purpose he has especially framed a pattern of prayer with such harmony and accord. He principally requires our prayers to be universal so that a few might meet together in his name and agree among themselves for what they will ask (Matt. 18:19). Yet because we are commanded to pray in secret, privately in our chamber, when we say "our Father," it is required that everyone apply that universal promise of the Fatherhood to himself. For Thomas said properly, "My Lord and my God!" (John 20:28) and Paul says,

"I thank my God..." (Rom. 1:8). So everyone in this way will conclude and say, "God is my Father." "Have you not just called to me: 'My Father...' " (Jer. 3:4). "How gladly would I treat you as my sons... 'I thought you would call me 'Father'" (Jer. 3:19). " Pray to your Father, who is unseen. Then your Father, who sees what is done in secret, will reward you" (Matt. 6:6).

Many profitable ideas are taught us in the few words of the preface to the Lord's Prayer. We may also think on these ideas by remembering the gifts that God has given us until now. God may, as it were, be moved to give, and by this giving our confidence is increased and confirmed so that we desire more necessary things. Since by his mere grace he has given us the main gift of adoption, and because he will be our Father and will be addressed that way, he will give us other things we need.

Chapter 3

"WHO ART IN HEAVEN"

Because "are" is a state-of-being verb, there are some who profusely speak about the immutable essence and the names of God, "I am that I am" and "which is, which was, and which is to come." But the Greek words neither require nor allow this argument. The words are plain. "Our Father, who art in heaven" shows that we do not call upon any earthly father but upon him who is or who dwells in heaven, that is, a heavenly Father. Christ himself explains these words when he called him a heavenly Father (Matt. 6:26). Heaven in Scripture is called the throne, seat, mansion, or dwelling place of God. In this place we call upon our Father who is in heaven. The meaning is not that the infinite essence of God is bound or included either in the visible heavens or in the highest heavens, as if he were not present everywhere. It is written that the heaven and the highest heavens cannot contain him (1 Kings 8:27; 2 Chron. 2:6). He fills heaven and earth (Jer. 23:24). Yes, he is present in heaven, on earth, in the sea and in hell (Ps. 139:7–9). He is higher than heaven, deeper than hell, wider than the earth, broader than the sea. This means that he is totally present everywhere. He is within all things and without all things as Gregory says. Neither do we think, when we call upon our Father who is in heaven, in the preface of this prayer, that he is separated or distant from us who pray. He is not distant from our wants or from our prayers like the heaven is far away from the earth. These are the ideas and the words of the wicked as described in Job 22:13. What can God see? Not that he walks in the circle of the heavens and does not think about our affairs. For in Psalm 145:18 it is written, "The LORD is near to all who call on him, to all who call on him in truth." "But if from there you seek the LORD your God, you will find him if you look for him with all your heart and with all your soul" (Deut. 4:29). "For where two or three come together in my name, there am I with them" (Matt. 18:20).

Now whereas our Father, whom we believe considers our requests, is said to be in heaven, the teachers speak about it in the following ways. First, the works of God as seen in the visible or material heavens appear more glorious and higher in beauty, magnificence, harmony, and workmanship than the works of God seen on earth. Second, in those spiritual heavens (as teachers call them), he does by a full communication of himself declare, exhibit, and show all his glory, power, goodness, and magnificence. It is not like here on earth, where he communicates by certain means, unseen signs, and vague sounds, but rather in full show and sight, face-to-face, to be seen and enjoyed by both the blessed angels and the elect souls. There we see the happiness, joy, salvation, and eternal life of the saints.

I cannot see what comfort this meaning affords for us who in weakness pray with all of the crosses here on earth. A simpler explanation is this: The Scriptures define heaven as where God has his abode, not in a local sense, but in a heavenly sense. There we see his divine glory, majesty, power, and fidelity. Therefore, because all things are under his government, God is said to be in heaven, to dwell in the heavens, to be in the place of his abode, to hear in the dwelling place of his abode (1 Kings 8:30). He has all things in his hands and in his power. He rules all things in all places. He is able to do and does whatsoever he will. By his wisdom he foresees, knows, beholds, and hears all things. He knows the way to help all who pray in weakness. By his providence he cares for all. By his power he orders, disposes, administers, and governs all things. "Our God is in heaven; he does whatever pleases him" (Ps. 115:3). "The LORD has established his throne in heaven, and his kingdom rules over all" (Ps. 103:19). "Then hear in heaven, your dwelling place. Forgive and act; deal with each man according to all he does, since you know his heart (for you alone know the hearts of all men)" (1 Kings 8:39). "Who is like the LORD our God, the One who sits enthroned on high, who stoops down to look on the heavens and the earth" (Ps. 113:5–6). "The LORD looked down from his sanctuary on high, from heaven he viewed the earth, to hear the groans of the prisoners and release those condemned to death" (Ps. 102:19–20). "The LORD is in his holy temple; the LORD is on his heavenly throne. He observes the sons of men; his eyes examine them" (Ps. 11:4). "He answers him from his holy heaven with the saving power of his right hand" (Ps. 20:6). "Look down from heaven and see from your lofty throne, holy and glorious" (Is. 63:15). When the Lord shows his divine glory, power and mercy by any famous healing,[1] help, and deliverance, the Scripture says that God has exalted or elevated himself above the heavens. He has enlarged his mercy even up to the heavens (Ps. 57:5, 18:5ff.). "His glory [is] above the heav-

---

1. The 1598 text has "hearing."

ens" (Ps. 113:4). "Sing praise to the Lord, to him who rides the ancient of skies above" (Ps. 68:33).

These testimonies of Scripture plainly explain the phrase in which God is said to be or to dwell in heaven. Further consideration of this will explain the doctrine of Christ's exaltation by his ascension into heaven and his session at the right hand of God in heaven. The meaning of this preface of the Lord's Prayer is evident. When we say "Our Father," we by faith think about the readiness, willingness, and eagerness of God to help us. When we add "who art in heaven," we add to the good will of God the following 1) divine power, that having all things in his power he is able to do and to give those things we ask; 2) divine providence, that seeing and knowing our wants, he is aware of our requests and hears the same; that he cares for us; that he orders, disposes, administers, and governs all things, especially all things in his Church; 3) divine wisdom, that he knows the way to send help and deliverance; and 4) divine rule and dominion, that it belongs to the kingdom and office of him who dwells in heaven to hear our prayers, to regard our affairs, to help, to deliver, and so forth. In other words, the Lord's Prayer says that our Father, upon whom we call, is or dwells in heaven. We should therefore never focus our minds on any common or earthly thing as God. This is the way of this world.

We also see here a comparison and a difference between an earthly father and our heavenly Father. Christ expressly sets them in opposition. "And do not call anyone on earth 'father,' for you have one Father, and he is in heaven" (Matt. 23:9). We also say that our Father dwells in heaven to show that by this title we are urged to ask God especially for heavenly things. When we ask for earthly things we are to ask that even these direct us heavenward. For we are called and born anew to an inheritance that is laid up in heaven, as it is written in 1 Peter 1:3–4. The title "Father" also shows that we are to be taught 1) to acknowledge our life in this world as a pilgrimage from God; 2) to enliven our hope of arriving in the true heavenly country; and 3) to frame our prayer so that, whatsoever we ask, our request brings us to the country where our Father is, that is, to heaven. The allegory of Augustine and others says that God is in heaven where, by grace, he dwells in the saints, who teach us that those who pray ought to ask God to dwell also in them. This is not impious, but in this case, it does not fit. It belongs to the second petition that God's kingdom may come unto us.

Specific petitions follow in this prayer. For it is not a true prayer when we only heap up the glorious titles of God. Prayer ought to ask something of God or else give thanks for gifts that have been received (Phil. 4:6; 1 Tim. 2:1). Usually there are seven numbered petitions. These are general signs and seals that refer to the categories under which we must find all those things for which we ask. For it is written in 1 John 5:14, "This is the confidence we have in approaching God: that if we ask anything according to his will, he hears us." "When you ask, you do not receive because you do it with the wrong motives, that you may spend what you get on your pleasures" (James 4:3). Therefore out of the petitions of this Lord's Prayer, which is the rule of praying, we may gather what things we are to ask in prayer in what order and for what end must ask them. They are thus divided that the first petitions address the glory of God, especially as it is joined with our salvation. The rest contain our wants, our blessings, and our salvation. Some of these belong to the body, others to the soul. Some belong to this worldly life, some to our spiritual life in this world, and others to our heavenly life to come. Some petitions require the giving and granting of blessings that are to come, either temporal and bodily or spiritual and heavenly. Other petitions desire the removal of evils either temporal or spiritual.

Evil is dealt with in three ways: 1) those evils that are past may be forgiven and not imputed, 2) those evils that are present may be taken away or lessened, and 3) those evils that are to come may be kept back. In the Lord's Prayer we desire both the purpose of prayer, that is, the glory of God, and also our own salvation and those things that impinge on it.

The Lord's Prayer also shows the order of those things for which we are to ask. First, we should ask for those things that concern the glory of God and our own salvation. Second, we ought to ask for the things that belong to the needs, wants, and functions of our bodies and of this life, as it is good for us to do so. Likewise the removal of those evils that hinder the glory of God or our salvation must stand in first place. Then we may pray that the adversities, tribulations, difficulties, and troubles of this body and of this life may either be taken away or lessened. Temporal or bodily gifts must be asked for with the condition or moderation: "If it be the will of God and if they will further the glory of God and our salvation." But when God knows and judges those things to be harmful for us, even though we think them to be good and profitable by asking for them, he should not give them to us or he should at least lessen the evilness of them. Temporal blessings must be asked for the purpose that they may be ordered, directed, and used to God's glory and to spiritual, heavenly, and eternal blessings.

From the petitions of the Lord's Prayer one may properly ascertain, that is, according to the will of God, what things for which we may and ought to ask and in what way. Likewise Paul in certain precise words shows and declares the kind of things that are to be asked for in prayer (Phil. 4:6; 1 Tim. 2:1). He divides prayer into petitions and thanksgiving. Petitions he divides into requests: 1) whereby we ask to receive blessings; 2) supplications, whereby we ask that evils be removed; and 3) intercessions, whereby we either ask and pray to God for the sake of others or else direct the weapons of our prayers against our enemies. Paul adds that the things to be prayed for are those dealing with the knowledge of God, our salvation and godliness, peace, and honesty in this life.

The Plan of Study

Now that we may quickly explain each of the distinct petitions, I will here outline the general topics from each pattern on which we should think when we pray. Accordingly, I have used them all for my private devotion and also for my public teaching of the Catechism. First of all, we consider by godly and devout meditation for what blessings we ask in every petition. We ask for the blessings to be given to us, and if they are already given, we ask that they may be preserved and increased. Second, in every petition we consider what evils we want stopped or prevented from happening. If they are to come or are present, we pray that they may be abated or that we may be freed and delivered from them. If they are abating, we pray that the evils may be removed even more quickly. Third, we meditate upon the blessings we are to acknowledge in every petition. We are to be thankful for those blessings. We ask that this confession and thanksgiving may be kindled, may grow, and may be increased in us. Fourth, in every petition and the items expounded therein, we must humble ourselves in confession; for we do not ask continually, earnestly, and fervently, but seldom and coldly. We should humbly confess that we do not sufficiently consider the greatness of them. We confess that, contrary to our words, we ourselves indeed refuse or repel those blessings for which we ask. Confession should also be made for the evils which we have done by word, which we pray against, and which by deed we attract and draw to ourselves. Confession is needed for the following reasons: 1) we do not acknowledge benefits received, 2) we are not heartily thankful for them, and 3) we forget them. We should confess that we do not appreciate them, nor do we use them reverently, that is, with thankfulness. It is not to God's glory when we ungratefully make them evil by our abuse of them.

In every petition with needful cries we are to acknowledge these things by humble confession. We must think upon all of this and by prayer seek to reform. All those things are to be applied both in general to the whole body of the Church, privately to ourselves, and by name also to those whose necessity we know. Through these acknowledgements we can meditate greatly on every petition. It is not my purpose at this time to handle them. I commend this task to every man's private devotion.

We will only expound the words in every petition and show the meaning of them all. We will briefly declare how they may and ought to be applied to those four questions or chief topics, namely: 1) what things for which we ask, 2) what evils we desire to be stopped or lessened, 3) how we are to be thankful, and 4) how we are to confess our unthankfulness and misuse.

Chapter 4

"HALLOWED BE THY NAME"

To discover the true meaning of this petition, we must explain the words. No doubt the praise, honor, and renown of God is treated here. For "name" is often taken for glory and renown. In Genesis 6:4, some are called men of name, whose fame was renowned. "He has declared that he will set you in praise, fame [name] and honor above all the nations he has made" (Deut. 26:19). The word "hallowed," as I shall soon show, is often used when anything is highly and gloriously renowned as famous. So that we may better consider the meaning of this petition in a godly manner, I will plainly divide the explanation into parts.

First, in general this petition commends us to desire God's glory. We should chiefly and before all things care for and seek the glory of God. We should consider all things for which we ask and all things we do to be done for the true goal of God's glory. This goal is to "do it all for the glory of God" (1 Cor. 10:31). Because of our corrupt nature we are not very careful about the true glory of God. For we find that those things that we do, those for which we ask, and those that we receive are not prayed for with much earnestness. Instead of giving God glory, we treat him with contempt and reproach. We profane, pollute, and blaspheme his name. Therefore, we are commanded to pray that God from heaven would kindle, preserve, and increase in us a true desire of God's glory. We pray also that we may be kept, defended, and delivered from all forgetfulness, contempt, profaning, defiling, and blaspheming of the name of God and of his glory.

Second, the name of God shows the properties of perfection, the attributes or virtues that God has revealed and declared in his Word concerning his essence, his will, and his works. He is wise, just, great, terrible, good, gentle, merciful, patient, penitent, jealous, visiting iniquity, and the like.

The Jews say the Hebrew word "Shem" because they will not pronounce the name "Jehovah" in its place. From this, the Chaldean paraphrase for God himself puts "Shem" as "Heshem," which means a name (Gen. 10:9). The virtues or perfection of God are the very essence of God. Now the name of God cannot be hallowed by any addition, infusion, access, or increase of holiness, as it is written of us, "let him who is holy continue to be holy" (Rev. 22:11). For the name of God is holy in itself. God's name is separated from all things. It excels and surpasses all other common and profane things in purity and holiness.

The word "holy" is used in Leviticus 10:3, for when the Lord had slain the two sons of Aaron, who had offered him unauthorized fire, he said, "Among those who approach me, I will show myself holy." For the vengeance taken upon Gog and Magog, he says, "I will show my greatness and my holiness" (Ezek. 38:23). After the threat of punishments, he says, "But the LORD Almighty will be exalted by his justice, and the holy God will show himself holy by his righteousness" (Is. 5:16). Speaking of the return of his people, he says, "But for the sake of my name I did what would keep it from being profaned in the eyes of the nations they lived among" (Ezek.

20:9). Of the punishment of Sidon and the deliverance of Israel, he says, "I will gain glory within you" (Ezek. 28:22). Concerning the return of his people, he says, "It is not for your sake, O house of Israel, that I am going to do these things, but for the sake of my holy name, which you have profaned among the nations where you have gone. I will show the holiness of my great name, which has been profaned among the nations, the name you have profaned among them. Then the nations will know that I am the LORD… when I show myself holy through you before their eyes" (Ezek. 36:22–23).

In this sense we pray that God would exhibit, show forth, and declare the glory and excellency of his name. His perfection and his attributes or virtues are shown in his name. This is done by great works either in his Church or against his enemies. His attributes may be specifically understood when every name of God is expounded. This I leave and commend to the private diligence of the reader. Since "Our Father" precedes "Hallowed be Thy name," we may properly understand the benefits of the person and office of the Father, the merits and benefits of the Son the Mediator, and the office and blessings of the Holy Ghost, which are revealed and made known in the Scripture as being subsumed under the word "name." These three things we desire to be hallowed, that is, mercifully to be declared and shown to us. The Scripture says that we must believe in the name of the only begotten Son so that we may receive remission of sins and eternal life in and by the name of Christ (John 3:16–18). If these things are separately explained, it will provide much reward. Here we explain only the chief topics for direction.

Third, by relation we desire that the name of God may be hallowed among us, with us, and by us. By this, we mean that God's attributes, which we said were understood in the name of God, might shine forth among us, become known in us, and be spread throughout all the world. Accordingly,

Scripture says, "I will gain glory within you. They will know that I am the LORD" (Ezek. 28:22). That we are forbidden to stain, to profane, or to blaspheme the name of God is shown most plainly in that it is to be hallowed or sanctified and not anything done to the contrary. We pray, therefore, that God would give us grace to acknowledge, to consider, to reverently propound and to spread about the works of God in our thought, word, and deed. For it is written in Psalm 48:10, "Like your name, O God, your praise reaches to the ends of the earth." The essential and personal virtues of God ought to be enlarged in this work. By this petition we desire that we may with holiness and reverence think and speak of the works and judgments of God. We desire that we may not be evil or envious petitioners. We should not wrongfully or smugly criticize either his goodness or his chastisements toward us. Nor should we criticize his long-suffering toward our enemies by complaining and murmuring against his works. By this we abuse his goodness, his gentleness, and his patience. When Moses and Aaron doubted God could give them water, the Lord said, "You did not trust in me enough to honor me as holy in the sight of the Israelites" (Numb. 20:12). "Do not be frightened. But in your hearts set apart Christ as Lord" (1 Pet. 3:14–15).

Fourth, the name of God is about his essence, his will, his works, and his judgments. His name is made known to us in the Word. We pray that the name of God, that is, his Word, may be given and preached to us purely, sincerely, in true and sound understanding, and in a holy manner. We also ask that it be preached without corruption and belittling. We also ask that we may be given sincere and faithful ministers so that the Church may be edified, and we ask that they be given the necessary gifts to faithfully do their duty. On the contrary we ask to be mercifully kept and preserved from wolves and hirelings who corrupt and defame the Word of God.

Fifth, remembering that through the Word of God he is made known, we must acknowledge the giving of the Word as the holy and singular blessing of God. We must reverently receive it and with diligence and devotion hear, think, and meditate on it. We must also sanctify and adorn the Word with a godly life. For if we do not, the name and doctrine of God may be polluted and spoken of as evil. However, we pray that others, by our godly conversation and life, may be drawn to love and embrace this doctrine (1 Tim. 6:1ff). "That they may see your good deeds and praise your Father in heaven" (Matt. 5:16). "Do you dishonor God by breaking the law? As it is written: 'God's name is blasphemed among the Gentiles because of you' " (Rom. 2:23–24).

Now let all these parts be applied to the four general topics before set down: 1) what blessings we desire to be given us, to be preserved, and increased; 2) from what evils we desire to be kept and delivered; 3) what blessings we must acknowledge as having been bestowed on us, and what thanks we ought to render again for them; and 4) what manner of confession of sins we must make in this petition. Let these be applied especially to the whole Church, in particular to ourselves and to those whose needs we know. If this is done, one will see that mediation on this petition will be very extensive.

Chapter 5

"THY KINGDOM COME"

In Greek this petition is simply "come." But because in Luke 11:20 it is written "The kingdom of God has come to you," it is not wrongly translated from the Latin as "Let the Kingdom come to you." Moreover, the kingdom of God is taken in many ways. In the general or universal kingdom of God, he mightily governs all creatures. "His kingdom rules over all" (Ps. 103:19). "Your kingdom is an everlasting kingdom" (Ps. 145:13). This we cannot thoroughly understand, for this kingdom runs mightily over all. Nothing can hinder it. No creature can remove itself from under it. We understand our prayer in this way: that all men may acknowledge, observe, and reverence the governance of the kingdom of God. For in this he rules, governs, and disposes all things. We therefore pray that we may humbly subject ourselves to it in all things.

Likewise the kingdom of grace in the Church in this life and the kingdom of glory in the life to come also exist and are here properly understood, the preface itself shows this. We say "Our Father…, thy kingdom come." This is called the kingdom of the Father, the kingdom of Christ, and the kingdom of heaven. To emphasize more the free gift of God, we do not say that we come to the kingdom of God, but rather pray that it may come to us. For Christ speaks more plainly, "The kingdom of God has come to you" (Luke 11:20). Now the kingdom of grace is "not a matter of eating and drinking, but of righteousness, peace and joy in the Holy Spirit" (Rom. 14:17). It consists not in speech but in truth and in power (1 Cor. 2:5). We pray, therefore, that the Holy Ghost may be given to us and that he may be powerful in us by the Word.

This Word is to illuminate, to convert, to justify, to sanctify, to lead, to guide, to confirm, and to preserve us. We pray that we may be found in that kingdom, there abide, and be preserved. For if we are not found there, we may fall away from it and again slide back into the kingdom of Satan. We pray that God would set his own kingdom against the kingdom of Satan and of the world. We ask that he would keep back and bind the Devil and that he would suppress, beat down, and break the treachery and the power of the Devil and of the world. We pray that he would mercifully defend and keep his Church from the same. With the psalmist in Psalm 110:2, we ask that "The LORD will rule in the midst of [our] enemies" and that he "will soon crush Satan under [our] feet" (Rom. 16:20). "Protect them from the evil one" (John 17:15) our Lord asks, so that "everyone born of God overcomes the world" (1 John 5:4; John 16:33). We ask him "to rescue us from the present evil age" (Gal. 1:4). Paul says, "Do not let sin reign in your mortal body so that you obey its evil desires" (Rom. 6:12). We ask that the Lord "let no sin rule over" us (Ps. 119:133) and that "those who belong to Jesus Christ have crucified the sinful nature with its passions and desires" (Gal. 5:24).

We pray that we may become subject to the direction of the Holy Ghost, be transformed by him into the obedient child of God, and become servants of righteousness. We should never answer this way: "We don't want this man to be our king" (Luke 19:14) or " 'Let us break [our] chains'… 'and throw off [our] fetters' " (Ps. 2:3). Rather, we take his yoke upon us because his yoke is sweet and easy. We do this so that we may find rest for our souls, that suffering and being heavy-laden we may fly to the throne of his kingdom and there be refreshed (Matt. 11:29; Heb. 4:16). We should "seek first his kingdom and his righteousness" (Matt. 6:33) that we may sit down in the kingdom of heaven and not be cast out (Matt. 8:11). We ask that we are not offenses in the kingdom of God (Matt. 18:6) or that the kingdom of God be not taken away from us (Matt. 21:43). Our prayer is that the kingdom of God may be within us (Luke 17:21) and that Christ may remember us in his kingdom (Luke 23:42). We also pray that this kingdom may continually be spread further abroad so that it may also come to other nations and countries. We desire more men to be gathered into that kingdom as time goes by. To be concise, we pray that we may earnestly say, "Blessed is the coming kingdom of our father David! Hosanna in the highest!" (Mark 11:10) and that we may receive that kingdom (Luke 19:15) and be made and remain citizens with the saints and the household of God (Eph. 2:19).

Concerning the kingdom of glory, we pray that God would make us fit to be partakers of the inheritance of the saints in light (Col. 1:12). We also pray that we may inherit and possess that kingdom by the grace of adoption (Matt. 25:34; 1 Cor. 15:50) and be mercifully kept and preserved from all things that may hinder us from the entrance and possession of the kingdom (2 Tim. 4:18). Peter says that we should love, wait for, and desire the coming of the kingdom of glory and hurry toward it (2 Pet. 3:12). We pray that we may be counted worthy of the kingdom of God (2 Thess. 1:5), for he has called us into his kingdom and glory (1 Thess. 2:12). He has made an entrance into the everlasting kingdom of God for us (2 Pet. 1:11). Finally, we pray that we may be ready at the coming of the kingdom (Luke 12:40).

These things we must ask in general for the whole body of the Church, privately for ourselves as well as for those whom we know, both friends and enemies. Likewise we must apply this petition to those four chief topics previously set down: 1) what good things we are to pray for in this petition, 2) what evils we are to pray against, 3) for what benefits we are to give thanks, and 4) what sins of ours we must humbly acknowledge and confess in this petition.

Chapter 6

"THY WILL BE DONE"

The will of God is taken in varying ways. Therefore, by making distinct divisions in God's will, we can easily understand the meaning of this petition. Ancient writers call one will of God the will of his good pleasure, disposition, or decree by which he himself wills and decides to do anything. Our will is weak even when we are strong and it is often hindered by other things. For this reason we have need to pray that God would give us strength to do the good things we think about in our own heart. Also we pray that he would remove all impediments so that we may do them. We need not pray concerning this will of God because he is almighty. Neither can we pray for it properly or in a godly manner. God does whatsoever he wills in heaven and in earth (Ps. 115:3). Who has resisted his will (Rom. 9:19)? "The word of the Lord stands forever" (1 Pet. 1:25). "For the LORD Almighty has purposed, and who can thwart him? His hand is stretched out; and who can turn it back?" (Is. 14:27). "What I have planned, that will I do" (Is. 46:11).

Another revealed or stated will is called the *known will of God*. When God commands or forbids anything in the Law or the Gospel, he shows and states what he will have us do and/or leave undone (Rom. 12:2). This is called the good will of God, his well-pleasing and perfect will. In this petition we acknowledge and confess that by our own strength we cannot do or fulfill the will of God, nor can we do that which is taught us in the Law or the Gospel.

We pray, therefore, that God would give us the spirit of regeneration and sanctification that may create in us a new heart, take away our stony heart, and subdue and abolish our carnal stubbornness and impatience. This is done so that we may think upon, desire, will, and do such things that please God. We also desire to avoid and omit those things that are contrary to his good will. If we find ourselves not regarding, not approving, not willing, not doing those things that God wills, but those things that God forbids, hates, and abhors, we pray that those things may be corrected in us by his Holy Spirit. This is done in true repentance so that our will may be turned from evil and be conformed to that which is good.

Altogether unlike and even resisting the will of God is the will of the Devil, the world, and the flesh. This we renounce and reject in this petition. We pray that the will of the world and the Devil may be hindered and subdued to the point that the suggestions of Satan may be stopped. Our prayer is that we may neither obey them nor conform ourselves to the world. We desire that the lusts and concupiscence [that is, the inborn inclination to sin] of our flesh may be crucified and mortified by the Spirit. We ask that, having the disobedience, the impatience, and the wicked lust of the flesh suppressed in us, our will may become conformed to the will of God. We ask to be moved to desire, covet, or do nothing but that which is wellpleasing and approved by God. Finally, we ask that we may reverently respect the will of God and submit ourselves to it, namely, that the will of God may be done in us. The

Scripture contains the good will of God in these three points: 1) "I take no pleasure in the death of the wicked, but rather that they turn from their ways and live" (Ezek. 33:11); 2) "For my Father's will is that everyone who looks to the Son and believes in him shall have eternal life" (John 6:40); and 3) "It is God's will that you should be sanctified, that you should avoid sexual immorality" (1 Thess. 4:3). Therefore we ask God for grace, strength, and aid that we may begin and accomplish the works of repentance, belief, and amendment of life.

Another will of God is called his *causitive or permitting will*. Whatsoever is done in all the world and in the Church cannot happen apart from God's either working or permitting it. Whatsoever befalls us is sure to come and cannot happen without the will of God either working or permitting it (Matt. 10:29). We do not approve of this will of God in our reason but rather we complain about it through impatience, murmuring, and resistance. Because of these complaints, we pray for patience that we may, with reverence and obedience, submit or at least endeavor to submit our will to the will of God. We pray that we may strive against impatience, not judging maliciously those things that happen to us by the will and permission of God. We are to say, "The Lord does whatever pleases him" (Ps. 135:6). Because we cannot do this of our own strength, we pray especially that God would give us patience, submission, obedience, strength, and courage in place of our impatience. Even for those things for which we ask, which seem to us very convenient, right, and profitable, we must always receive them as the will of God. "Not my will, but yours be done" (Luke 22:42).

Others make an *optative will* of God, whereby he shows the very fact that he wishes and desires those things that are profitable and wholesome for us. This we ourselves often hinder by an opposite action. For example, it is said that God will have "all men to be saved and to come to a knowledge of the truth" (1 Tim. 2:4). "How often I have longed to gather your children together…, but you were not willing" (Matt. 23:37). "I take no pleasure in the death of the wicked, but rather that they from their ways and live" (Ezek. 33:11). "[N]ot wanting anyone to perish, but everyone to come to repentance" (2 Pet. 3:9). Therefore, we pray that this will of God may be mercifully fulfilled in us. We pray that it will not be removed from us by the suggestions of Satan, by the allurements of the world, or by the concupiscence [that is, the inborn inclination to sin] of the flesh.

When the prayer says "on earth, as it is in heaven," it is a Hebrew figure of speech that is more properly expressed like this: "even as it is in heaven, so also in earth." Chrysostom thinks that this clause is to be referred to each of the former petitions: "Hallowed be thy name; thy kingdom come, on earth as it is in heaven.…" Here we have a very good opportunity to consider what Paul says, that in Christ all things in heaven and on earth are reconciled and set at one [Col. 1:20]. There shall be one company of blessed angels and men [Heb. 12:22–23]. Christ also says that we shall become "like the angels" [Mark 12:25].[1] We are therefore taught to pray that this unity between the company of angels and of men may be begun in this life. We desire that we may progress toward and seek after that blessed communion. The angels readily and cheerfully, without any stubbornness and resistance, but out of love and obedience, execute those things which they know are God's will, as it is said in Psalm 103:20–21: "you his angels, you mighty ones who do his bidding, who obey his word… who do his will." Therefore, we pray that this also may be begun in us. We are admonished, considering we belong to this communion, that we should conform ourselves to it and not to the world. We are not of this world but belong to a heavenly city. Now this conformity or likeness is begun in this life

---

1. The reference for the Mark quotation along with the previous Colosians and Hebrews quotations are purposely placed in brackets. Chemnitz uses references in the 1598 text extensively. These three are the only references throughout this edition which are not in the 1598 edition. They are inserted merely for the convenience of the current reader.

but will be perfected only in the life to come, which is eternal.

Further, the angels think reverently on the judgments of God and in all things approve of that which God wills. We also desire that, by the grace of God and by the workings of his Spirit, we may do the same here on earth. So this clause "thy will be done" contains a very profitable admonition that, while we live in the flesh here on earth, we should begin to lift up our heads and our souls. We should begin to desire and think of our life in heaven with the blessed angels. We should labor to begin our conformity with them here on earth.

Again, this exposition is to be applied to those four topics of godly devotions and meditation: 1) what blessings we are to desire in this petition, 2) what evils we are to pray against, 3) for what benefits we must give thanks, and 4) what contrary sins of ours we must acknowledge and confess. This should be done either in general for the whole Church or in particular for ourselves and others.

Chapter 7

"GIVE US THIS DAY OUR DAILY BREAD"

So that we may come to the true meaning of this petition, we must first expound the words. To begin, the word translated as "bread" properly means ordinary bread for food. This bread is cut and chewed; often it is distinctly named "bread or… water" (1 Kings 13:9), "bread and wine" (Gen. 14:18), and "grain and bread" (Gen. 45:23). By a metonymy it is taken for grain from which bread is made (Gen. 47:13; Ps. 104:15). By a synecdoche it is taken for any kind of meat, as in he "set food and water before them so that they may eat and drink" (2 Kings 6:22–23). It is likewise taken for the whole banquet, both food and drink as in "to eat" (Luke 14:1; Ex. 18:12). Goat's milk is called bread (Prov. 27:27), as is the root of juniper. Even feed for cattle (Ps. 147:9) and the fruit of trees (Jer. 11:19) are called bread. The word "bread" in this petition encompasses all things belonging to and necessary for the sustenance of this body and life.

Our Savior Christ in Matthew 6:25, Jacob in Genesis 28:20, and Paul in 1 Timothy 6:8 use this meaning in the phrase "food and clothes." Those means by which food and clothes are obtained, such as farming, trading, and the like, are included in the name "bread" (Prov. 31:14). In this petition our Savior Christ includes all bodily things that are required for a comfortable life. Isaac prays for his wife (Gen. 25:21) and the centurion prays for his servant (Matt. 8:6). Paul commands us to pray for the magistrate "that we may live peaceful and quiet lives in all godliness and holiness" (1 Tim. 2:2). Solomon prays for seasonable weather and for the fruitfulness of the earth (1 Kings 8:36). Therefore, the word "bread" in this petition may be properly understood in a large sense for all those things that are required for the necessary, peaceable, and honest ordering of this life. This applies to the nation, the family, the productivity of the ground, profitable weather, and so on.

Further, whereas Christ calls this bread "daily," there is no agreement as to what that word properly signifies. Before Jerome's time, the Latin translation had "bread for this day" because, without any doubt, Luke adds "this day." Jerome[1] translated it as referring to the Heavenly Bread that gives life, the Bread of Super Substance, namely Christ. Ambrose agrees with Jerome in the *Fifth Book of the Sacraments*, adding that it is not the bread that goes into the body, but the bread of eternal life (John 6:48) that sustains the substance of the soul.[2] The Hebrew word signifies our own proper goods or a peculiar treasure. Symachus translated this word as "chief," "singular," or "peculiar." The Septuagint translated it as "daily proper needs." Because of these variations Ambrose thinks these two different words, peculiar and proper, must be unified to mean that which excels all substances and creatures, namely,

1. Jerome, "Against the Pelagians," Book 3, paragraph 15.

2. Ambrose, "De Sacramentis," *Patrologiae Cursus Completus Patrologiae Latinae*, accurante J. P. Migne, XVI (Paris: Apud Garnier Fratres, 1880), p. 471.

Christ. Cyprian,[3] Jerome, Ambrose,[4] and Augustine understand it as the substance of the Lord's Body.

Ambrose adds and Jerome openly shows that "daily" can also mean "tomorrow," for the Greeks call the day coming or tomorrow "daily" (Acts 7:26). Xenophon uses the same word in the phrases "in the current or present year" and "in the winter following." Those things that are to come are called "daily." Demosthenes, in writing against Midias, calls the next assembly following, "daily." I have also studied this word in the Septuagint and have found it used in this sense in Deuteronomy 32:29: "Discern what their end will be." This word is also used in 1 Chronicles 20:1: "in the spring." In Proverbs 27:1 it is used obviously to mean the next coming day: "Do not boast about tomorrow, for you do not know what a day may bring forth." In the Hebrew it is simply "day," and the Greeks translate it as "necessities coming tomorrow," next following, or ensuing. Jerome further adds that he has found in the Gospel according to the Hebrews the word "day," which signifies tomorrow or the day to come, used in the place of the Greek word "daily."

Erasmus holds this same sense. Because Christ forbids us to worry about the temporal cares of tomorrow, Erasmus explains that Christ commanded us to ask not for bread in the present life, but food for the life to come. He gives this reason: It is not like Christ to ask in so spiritual a prayer for corporal bread from his heavenly Father; even the heathen receive this from their parents. This reason of Erasmus is wrong because God will have us depend on him not only for our spiritual care but for all our cares (1 Pet. 5:7). Our heavenly Father knows that we have need even of these temporal things (Matt. 6:23). He will have us acknowledge that it is he who gives us those things that are included in daily food. He is angry if

---

3. Cyprian, "On the Lord's Prayer," Treatise IV, paragraph 18.

4. Ambrose, "De Sacramentis," p. 471.

anyone should think that they have received these things from somewhere else rather than from him (Hosea 2:8; Joel 2:23). He has also commanded us to ask these things of him (1 Kings 8:35). Jacob in Genesis 28:20 and Solomon in Proverbs 30:7–8 have asked for these things in prayer. Seeing that the Lord's Prayer is a perfect form of prayer containing all things God will have us ask of him, it is necessary that there should be some place for daily bread. It is not found in any other petition, it is found here. It would be a great impiety either to ascribe those things concerning our proper daily care to a creature or to our own work. We are not even to ask for them in a prayer to the saints.[5] By asking them of the saints we would not think of our daily bread as the gift of God.

Therefore, the word for "tomorrow's receipts" may well mean daily bread. It is not understood in the sense of "one's own property," but the theme thereof is a verb and a gerund, which emphasize the movement in the phrase "to come to." Since Plutarch uses the word "daily" in the *Life of Sertorius*, "daily coming from house to house," so it follows that daily bread is that food which comes to us as a gift from someone other than ourselves. This bread cannot be received only once, but because times are always changing, we must have it come to us new each and every day, that is, continually. Luke calls the food that surrounds us and comes to us every day from the hand of God "our daily bread" (Luke 11:3). Hesiod uses the word even more broadly in calling it food sufficient and necessary for a whole year. Plutarch,[6] in the *Life of Pericles*,

---

5. One might conclude from this statement that Chemnitz did not oppose praying to the saints, which stands in opposition to the Apology of the Augsburg Confession, Article XXI, section 31 (Theodore G. Tappert, *The Book of Concord* [Philadelphia: Fortress Press, 1979], p. 233). Since this is a translation and not a commentary, it is not appropriate to change Chemnitz' observations in this matter. Chemnitz was, however, one of the theologians who helped produce the writings that became the Apology of the Augsburg Confession (*ibid.*, Preface to the Book of Concord, p. 7, fn. 7) and thus it is likely that his reference to praying to the saints addresses an audience whose traditions and tendencies he well knew, since historically prayer to the saints was commonplace for the believers to whom Chemnitz had been ministering.

6. Plutarch, "The Life of Pericles," *The Harvard Classics*, XII (New York: P. F. Collier and Sons, 1909), p. 403.

calls it food for each day. Sometimes "daily" signifies time that keeps on giving. This meaning may be that now and then, as time goes on in this life, we have a continual need of this bread. In this action it is to teach us that our heavenly Father feeds us continually by making a new supply of bread every day. It may also be understood that this bread is not called bread sought out of need but, as Varinius calls it, surplus bread. It teaches us that we should not credit it to our own work but to the gift of God. It might teach us that bread is not the principle thing for which we must ask of God in prayer. But in this we ask for a surplus or a thing that comes in addition to the necessary thing. "Seek first his kingdom and his righteousness and all these things will be given to you as well" (Matt. 6:33). Because adjectives ending in this way need to be grammatically formed with participles of the feminine gender, the most plain and safest way is to define this word as a substance, "daily bread," which is necessary for the sustenance of our body and our new life.

Basil, in his *Short Questions*, explains "daily bread" as that which is good and profitable for preserving our daily life. Suidas says "daily bread" is bread that fits properly with our life or bread that we use every day. Theophilact explains it as bread that is sufficient for our life and well-being. Euthymius repeats the same thing, that it is bread that keeps us alive and functioning properly, adding moreover that Chrysostom explains it as that bread which is needed daily.

Furthermore, "daily bread" also can mean possessions or money. "Give me my share of the estate" (Luke 15:12). From this usage two words are derived. One, as has been said, means a peculiar, special, or proper treasure and the other, which is opposite, means a generic, necessary, and sufficient amount of money. The Syrian translator expressed it as a word that we should understand as meaning necessary bread that we need. John the Baptist uses the same word when he says, "I need to be baptized by you" (Matt. 3:14). "Daily bread," taken in this sense, will very properly agree with that which is written in Proverbs 30:8, "Give me neither poverty nor riches," that is, feed me with bread ordained or set aside for me or with the bread custom baked for me. The Greeks translate these words as "give me those things which are needful and sufficient. Give me just enough." "Godliness with contentment is great gain" (1 Tim. 6:6). I thought it good to note these things here as being worthy of consideration by the learned. In doing so the meaning of this petition is more plainly shown forth.

In this petition, therefore, we are admonished and taught that men's affairs in this common outward life do not unfold rashly and occur by chance. Bodily goods, outward wealth, and whatsoever belongs to the happy estate of the government or of the family do not depend upon the wisdom, diligence, and dexterity of men. They are not to be credited to blind chance, to fate, or to the course of secondary causes, but God himself plans and governs all these things according to his good pleasure. Unless God keeps the city and builds the house, men labor in vain (Ps. 127:1). In Daniel we find how the affairs of kingdoms are cared for by God. "Rich and the poor have this in common: The LORD is the Maker of them all" (Prov. 22:2). "The LORD will open the heavens; the storehouse of his bounty, to send rain on your land" (Deut. 28:12; cf. Ps. 135:8). We are not to think that God has given this task away, as if it were too lowly for his high majesty, nor may we think that he has turned the care of bodily, temporal, and earthly blessings over to the saints. He seriously affirms that prosperity and adversity even in these things come from him (Lev. 26:3; Deut. 28:12). He is angry if we do not acknowledge this (Hosea 2:8; Joel 2:23). Our Savior Christ ascribes to our heavenly Father the care of our souls, our bodies, our lives, our food, and raiment (Matt. 6:32). Therefore, we are commanded to ask him in prayer to give us these blessings and to remove and deliver us from harm. If these things happen to us, with great thanksgiving we are to acknowledge them as his special blessings. In all this we pray that God would take away from us all ungodly worrying, doubting, distrusting, and coveting so that we may be undoubtedly convinced that our heavenly Father is both willing and able to give daily bread unto his children. In quietness, this hope is our strength. Moses prays for the fruits of the earth (Deut. 26:15). In the stories in the Gospels, the diseased lepers, the blind, and others pray. Isaac in Genesis 25:21 and Hannah in 1 Samuel 1:11 pray against barrenness. Paul prays for magistrates (1 Tim. 2:2) and Jeremiah prays for the peace of the city (Jer. 29:7).

Because God will have us work and use ordinary ways of getting our daily bread, we pray that he would present opportunities for us and then bless them. We ask that he would profit those who plant and those who water (1 Cor. 3:6). "The blessing of the Lord brings wealth, and he adds no trouble to it" (Prov. 10:22). Because we are commanded to ask for daily bread, this asking teaches us that we may not pray for pleasures, for reserves, and for excess to use for sinning or for show. In other words, according to Solomon's interpretation (Prov. 30:8), we pray that we may not be burdened with too much wealth or oppressed with too much poverty. Solomon here adds that we also pray against those evils and sins that arise out of extremes either in wealth or in poverty. Likewise, according to Paul (Phil. 4:18; 1 Tim. 6:6), we pray for contentment and for a godly and wholesome use of every vocation. We ask that our soul may neither hate manna, nor desire the fleshpots of Egypt, nor view quails grudgingly (Numb. 11:5). We are to accept God's gift as his good will for us as he distributes the fishes among the crowd giving as much as he decides (John 6:11). As in the previous petitions, that the Father's will be done must also be considered with this petition. Now we call this "our bread," not because it is gotten by our own work or is owed to us by some kind of right, but because God of his goodness has determined and set up these things for the sustenance of this life. This is given to us as a free gift from God. Some receive their specific gift because it is necessary for the accomplishment of their vocation. God has determined what and how much he will give to everyone out of the treasury of his good pleasure.

Because Paul speaks against idleness and any unlawful means of getting food, he commands all to work so that everyone may eat his own bread (Eph. 4:28; 2 Thess. 3:8). It is also good for us to understand that our bread is not to be violently taken from others by wrong or gotten from others by idleness. It is written, "You shall eat the fruit of your labor" (Ps. 128:2). When we pray for "our bread," this petition teaches us to be mindful also for the needs of others. Yes, those things that are given to me and given to you are given to us so that we should give some of it to others (Eph. 4:28). It is not mine or yours, but "our" bread. Therefore, it is the poor man's bread that you keep when you do not give to the poor.

This bread for which we are commanded to pray is "daily" (Matt. 6:11). Luke says "each day" and "daily" to teach us that God takes care of us every moment. This very word "daily" serves as a bridle to all foolish and ungodly worry about tomorrow. This is done so that a man may restrain and moderate any excessive desire for the things of this life. All of us are troubled by this trait. We ought not think, when we have some goods and wealth stored up, that since we have this reserve we need not pray this petition. Even then we must use this prayer so that we may acknowledge this reserve to be the gift of God and ourselves to be the Lord's beggars.

Augustine says we should pray so that those things that have already been given to us may be kept safe. He reminds us also to pray that out of those things given to us, we may have what is needed for today, but especially with a blessing. In this God gives strength to the bread for the sustenance of this life and causes the use of it to be wholesome for us. We pray especially that as we use it, God would not have us eat and not be satisfied (Lev. 26:26). "I will cut off the supply of food in Jerusalem. The people will eat rationed food in anxiety and drink rationed water in despair" (Ezek. 4:16). This is also done so that we will not be found in the number of those who seek and receive their goods and their entire portion in this life and then are barred from the inheritance of heavenly and eternal blessings (Ps. 17:14; Luke 16:25). These people are prepared "for the day of slaughter" (Jer. 12:3).

The ancient writers, as may be gathered by their interpretations, put it simply as "daily" (Luke 11:3). Not all copies have the article "this." It therefore modifies not bread but rather that which will suffice each day continually. It can also be taken as bread that is sufficient for this day. This agrees with that which Matthew has, namely "today." Aristotle in *Politic.* 2 uses this word to signify daily food.

Our Savior Christ, while reminding us of this petition, has followed and foreshadowed this custom, in that before meals he blessed it and gave thanks (Matt. 14:19; Matt. 15:36; Luke 24:30). Therefore, Paul says that it is a doctrine of devils that commands people to "abstain from certain foods, which God created to be received with thanksgiving by those who believe and know the truth. For everything God created is good, and nothing is to be rejected if it is received with thanksgiving, because it is consecrated by the word of God and prayer" (1 Tim. 4:3–5). By "word" Paul understands that Word of God by which the use and government of the creatures, created for our good, was given to men in the beginning (Gen. 1:29). After it was lost by sin, it was restored again by the intercession of the Son (Gen. 9:2). Therefore the difference of meats is taken away in the New Testament (Col. 2:16), for "to the pure, all things are pure" (Titus 1:15). By prayer also he understands that when, as adopted children, we desire that our own bread may be given to us from the bountiful hand of our Father with his blessing, we ask that our use of it may please God. In doing so we ask that we may enjoy the same with joyful and good conscience. This also is the special gift of God, as Solomon says, "Eat and drink, and find satisfaction in all his toil" (Eccl. 3:13; Eccl. 5:18).

Thus are these things to be asked in general for the whole body of the Church, privately for ourselves, and namely for others whose needs we know. To do this we may apply this petition to the four general heads before set down: 1) what blessings we are to ask; 2) what evils we are to pray against that they may be removed, taken away, or that we may be delivered from them; 3) for what benefits we are to be thankful unto God; and 4) what sins of ours we must acknowledge and confess unto God in this petition for pardon and amendment.

Chapter 8

"FORGIVE US OUR DEBTS"

The petition for daily bread is not placed before the petition asking for the remission of sins as though money were to be sought after first and godliness learned after wealth is gotten. Our Savior Christ bids us to "seek first his kingdom and his righteousness" (Matt. 6:33). Because we by nature seek worldly goods, it is the will of God that the acknowledgment of his benefits should begin first in us as we receive earthly things and that through these we may meditate on the knowledge of God. Through this acknowledgment we may grow to desire spiritual and heavenly blessings. The ruler with all his family was brought to believe in Christ by the outward curing of his son (John 4:53). Jacob says, "If God will be with me on this journey I am taking and will give me food to eat and clothes to wear,… then the LORD will be my God" (Gen. 28:20–21). Therefore, the petition for bread is connected immediately to the petition for remission of sins. They are knit together by the conjunction[1] "and." This is to teach us

---

1. The 1598 text has "copulative particle."

to desire and care for those things that concern the eternal salvation of our souls with the same fervency of spirit that we earnestly desire and are naturally motivated to seek worldly goods. It is natural to desire bodily goods and wealth. The conjunction[2] "and" shows us that Christ withholds from and gives to us food. By this we are taught that we must pray to God for food. We must refer the giving and receiving of it to his good pleasure.

Those things that Matthew calls debts are referred to as sins by Luke. From this we may know how the word "debt" is to be understood in this place. It is a usual Chaldean figure of speech to use "to be indebted or bound to" to mean sins, offenses, and wickedness. Christ in his sermons often uses the word "debt" in place of "sins," as in the parable in Matthew 18:24. He does this in the story of the sinful woman (Luke 7:47) and again in Luke 13:2: "Do you think that these Galileans were worse sinners than all the other Galileans because they suffered this way?" Here, then, this phrase is to be noted as we consider what instructions we must learn from the fact that sins are called debts. For seeing that men make for themselves sins out of their private superstition, from the traditions of men, or from some Pharisaical challenge, namely to be just and perfect, the word "debt" leads us directly to the Law or Decalog. It moves us to the Law as the only place where the rule of God's justice is found.

The Law shows us what our nature ought to be, what we ought to do, and what we ought not to do. Plainly it tells us what perfection and purity are. Christ says, "we have only done our duty" (Luke 17:10). Paul says that we are debtors to live after the Spirit (Rom. 8:12–13). Because the Law is the statement of our debt to God, it shows us how many ways we amass such an exceedingly great debt. We do this by doing those things that we ought not do, by leaving undone those

---

2. The 1598 text has "conjunction copulative."

things that we ought to do, and by doing those things we do wrongly, imperfectly, and impurely. The same word can also mean a fault, a guiltiness, an offense, and condemnation. For example, when we do not pay a debt, we are condemned and given some kind of punishment. The Greeks used the word "to owe" as to owe a penalty or a fine, or to be condemned to die for a sum of money. Christ used this phrase when he said, "You may be thrown into prison… and will not get out until you have paid the last penny" (Matt. 5:25–26). Again he said, "Since he was not able to pay, the master ordered that he and his wife and his children and all that he had be sold to repay the debt" (Matt. 18:25). This phrase teaches us to ask forgiveness both of the guilt and of the punishment. In this we are different and reject the teaching of the Papists.

Already we have fully explained that the purpose of the Lord in dispensing temporal consequences often in this life, even after sin is forgiven, is not for punishment but rather for correction. The Lord commanded his Apostles and those who have God as their Father to pray for forgiveness of sin every day just as we pray daily for bread. This shows, against the Pelagians,[3] that no child of God is perfect and without sin in this life. Everyone has need every day to humble himself and to pray for forgiveness of his sins. It shows also, in opposition to the Novatians,[4] that those who sin after baptism and repentance may obtain forgiveness if they turn again and repent. Those who are baptized and reconciled to God are commanded to continually pray for the forgiveness of their sins. Look what great thing we ask in his name and by his commandment. He has promised on oath to give the same to us.

The use of this doctrine against the Pelagians puts us in mind of our own weakness every day and serves to bring us

---

3. The Pelagian movement was a series of controversies of the fourth and fifth centuries that in essence denied the doctrine of original sin and thereby made conversion a mere work of man. It places man's own good work as the source of eternal salvation.

4. The Novatians are members of a heretical sect in the early church who denied the availability of absolution to baptized Christians who sinned after their baptism.

to humility. On the other hand, this petition also shows that the mercy and pardon we are commanded to seek by prayer is not to be asked of the angels or of the saints but only of God himself. This is also to be asked only in the use of the means by which God will give remission of sins. Because we are commanded to pray for the forgiveness of our debts in this very prayer, we humbly confess before God that we cannot make sufficient payment or satisfaction for our sins. In this we stand in opposition to the Papist view of penance. We totally depend on free forgiveness for our Mediator's sake. Because our sins "have separated you from your God" (Is. 59:2), we desire in this petition the grace of God, his reconciliation and acceptance. Whoever looks for these things, either in satisfaction or in merit and not in the mere mercy of the Father, shall never see them. Whoever does not seek the payment, satisfaction, and merit of Christ alone does not properly seek them, neither shall he ever get them. We are commanded to ask for the forgiveness of our debts. The word "forgive" will not allow the thought that it is our payment, our work, or our satisfaction, but only allows forgiveness to be considered as a free gift. The Greeks translate the Hebrew word "forgiving" as "to be gracious, merciful, and pardoning." "The Lord our God is merciful and forgiving" (Dan. 9:9). "In accordance with your great love, forgive the sin of these people" (Num. 14:19).

Having explained these words, we may easily see for what we are to ask in this petition. We pray for forgiveness because our debts are innumerable, infinite, and immeasurable. We ask that God will not judge us by them and that he will not charge them to us. We ask that he will not charge them and require us to pay for them but for Christ's sake mercifully to pardon them (Is. 53:6). We ask him to "hurl all our iniquities into the depths of the sea" (Micah 7:19). The consequence of sin is the displeasure, wrath, or anger of God. The curse and condemnation of God brings the punishments of this curse upon our body and soul in this life, and in the life to come it brings eternal death. Therefore, we ask the Lord to remove his deserved wrath. We plead with him not to be enraged with us or pour out his wrath upon us, but to lay aside his anger and to embrace us with grace and mercy. We ask him to become and always to be a gracious and merciful Father toward us. We ask him not to reward us according to our sins, neither lay upon us the punishment of his curse, nor cast us into prison until we have made satisfaction (Matt. 5:25; 18:25), but to pardon both the guilt and the punishment of our sins. We ask him to set us free from the bondage or debt of our sin. In this way we say with Paul, "Who will bring any charge against those whom God has chosen?" (Rom. 8:33).

Since they are not generic debts or sins but rather "our debts," everyone who desires to pray this petition ought to consider the Ten Commandments of the Law. In each of them he should consider what sins he has committed. He must carefully examine whether they are sins of pride (Ps. 19:13) or sins of infirmity and weakness. In doing this we rightly know how to pray for pardon. Because sin is never forgiven unless we repent (Jer. 5:7), and we personally, because of our hard heart, are careless and cannot repent, we are at a loss for we do not judge, consider, or count our sins. We never consider how many, how great, and how grievous they are. We do not earnestly grieve for our sins or from our heart detest or forsake them. We do not turn from them but we take pleasure in our sins and boast about them like they did in Sodom (Is. 3:9). We neither fear God nor are we affected by the fear of God's wrath. Therefore, when we pray for the forgiveness of our sins, we ask that God by his Spirit would drive out of us all security. We ask that the Law will uncover all our hidden or covert sins. We beg that he would take from us our stony and impenitent heart and give us a living and repentant heart so that we may acknowledge and detest our own sins. We should desire to repent of our sin, understand the wrath of God, and fear him.

We also pray that he would strengthen us by true faith and preserve us from despair, for by faith we receive the forgiveness of sins. Because this petition for forgiveness of sins is joined by the conjunction "and" to the fourth petition, where we pray for daily bread for the day, we are commanded to pray this petition also every day. In this way we are reminded to be careful not to allow our sins to grow into so great a mound that we are to be found in the books of God's judgments (Dan. 7:10) without forgiveness. We must pray every day that our daily sins may be blotted out. Daily we must ask that they not be written with a pen of iron and that we are not "storing up wrath against [ourselves] for the day God's of wrath" (Rom. 2:5).

Because God has appointed and ordained certain means whereby he will bestow and whereby we must receive the forgiveness of sins, we likewise pray that God would give us such a mind that we do not condemn or neglect them but daily exercise the use of the keys of heaven. We ask that by the hearing of the Word, the use of the Sacraments, and other exercise of faith and prayer, God would not give us "over to a depraved mind, to do what ought not to be done" (Rom. 1:28; cf. Eph. 4:17).

Lastly, we pray that we may receive the remission and forgiveness of our sins before we die. We ask that before the end of this life we may use those means whereby the forgiveness of our sins may be normally given to us. There are so many and such great blessings we must meditate upon when we pray "forgive us our sins." In this we may plainly see what devotion and thought is required in the very act of prayer.

Now all these things we must ask for the whole body of the Church in general, privately for ourselves, and by name for those whose necessity we know, for we say "our debts or trespasses." Although the three later petitions are deprecatory, that is, in them we pray against evils, it is profitable to apply them to the four general types set down in the beginning. As we have shown that the former requesting petitions contained prayers against evils, thanksgivings, and confessions of sins, so there is the same reason in these deprecatory petitions. They contain petitions for blessings, thanksgivings, and confessions.

Chapter 9

"AS WE FORGIVE OUR DEBTORS"

In Luke one reads, "for we also forgive." Now we must not take the "as" of Matthew to be completely the same. We must not think that God should forgive with no more perfect measure of mercy than that with which we forgive others. The flesh fights against the Spirit in us even when we are reconciled to our neighbor. God himself shows the inequality between God's forgiveness and our forgiving, saying: "How can I treat you like Admah? How can I make you like Zeboiim?... I will not carry out my fierce anger... for I am God, and not man" (Hosea 11:8–9). Speaking of the most fervent love of a mother, God says, "Can a mother forget the baby at her breast?... I will not forget you!" (Is. 49:15). Neither does Luke go about trying to give the cause or reason by which and for which we deserve the forgiveness of sins, for it is the free grace of God proceeding out of his mere love and compassion for us (Matt. 18:27).

Paul uses the word "forgave." God of his free pleasure has pardoned us. He does not set in opposition our forgiving to God's forgiving as if it were bought at a price or earned. It is not as if God should forgive us because we have previously forgiven another. But he says, "Be kind and compassionate to one another, forgiving one another, just as in Christ God forgave you" (Eph. 4:32). "Bear with each other and forgive whatever grievances you may have against one another. Forgive as the Lord forgave you" (Col. 3:13). This phrase does not tell us the basis on which the pardon of God depends, but as Cyprian says, "It is a condition and pledge thereof."[1] For just as children are often made worse by parents correcting them too gently, so our corrupt flesh, hearing that God's pardon is always ready for those who pray to him for it and repent, will take liberty in this to sin more freely afterward hoping to obtain pardon easily. By doing this we abuse the endless benefits of God's free pardon, as though it were some filthy and unlawful liberty. By this clause Christ binds the intent and purpose of those who pray as if it were a public condition and promise. They will then be aware of all their sin, amend their lives, and seek to be godly.

It is therefore a weighty admonition, almost a vow or promise in the sight of our heavenly Father, that we do not abuse this fatherly gentleness and readiness to forgive by the liberty of sinning. We promise, as it were, a vow, an amendment of life. Christ teaches this general doctrine concerning the good purpose of the amendment of life with a special example of forgiving one another in a brotherly way. This very rightly agrees with the words of this petition, as we have said, concerning turning the other cheek (Matt. 5:39). The flesh is corrupt and has a core of bitterness (Heb. 12:15). It is of itself full of impatience, desires revenge, and persists in anger. It is very far from reconciliation and forgiveness.

---

1. Cyprian, "On the Lord's Prayer," Treatise IV, paragraph 18.

Therefore we also pray that this core of bitterness may be cut off, beaten down, and mortified in us by the Holy Ghost. We ask that a love of unity, of reconciliation, and of forgiveness may grow in us. We hope that the fact that we have not forgiven one another with all our heart, or in our heart have not wanted to forgive, may never be charged against us.

Because we can neither live in this world without many sins against the Lord nor live and work among our brethren without many offenses against each other, Christ joined both these together in this fifth petition. Since peace of conscience towards God is maintained by the continual forgiveness of sins, brotherly love, with which God is chiefly delighted, it cannot be preserved among us except by the continual reconciliation and forgiving of one another. Therefore, he joins brotherly pardoning with God's forgiving, as he shows in the parable [of the unmerciful servant] in Matthew 18:23 which clearly teaches this petition. He desires to forcibly break and correct the wicked impatience and bitterness of the heart. He wishes to upset the reasons we like to pretend are valid and give us the true right to take revenge. We like to pretend that we can properly compare our debt, which we as servants of God owe, with the debts of fellow servants. We like to argue that since our neighbor's sins are great and many, and since we ourselves have given many gifts and have been very considerate of our neighbor, we are as good as anyone since we all owe debts to someone. Either we are ignorant and unaware that we may have caused part of our own hurt when we feel our neighbor has hurt us, or else, being offended and hurt, we sin by being impatient and bitter.

James says, "Confess your sins to each other and pray for each other" (James 5:16). Lest we should be offended because our neighbor often offends us or we run out of patience when we have to keep on forgiving and reconciling so much, we have been taught that we must repeat every day to God the petition "Forgive us our debts." We do this that we might forgive our neighbor, "not seven times, but seventy-seven times" (Matt. 18:22). By this attitude and promise, "even as we also forgive," he does straightly motivate and urge us to desire to and be ready to forgive our brethren.

We should remind ourselves that we can negatively place in jeopardy our faith, solemnly given and bound in this petition. Unless we forgive our neighbor, we ask for God to be angry at us and withhold the love and the compassion of forgiveness. Chrysostom says, "We do not pray unto God but provoke him; we do not obtain favor but we pronounce the sentence of condemnation against ourselves. At the last judgment we shall be judged according to the sentence that we say: 'even as we also forgive.' " By this means, God is moved to take away and not give the benefit of the remission of sins, as the parable says in Matthew 18:34. It does no good to try to get out of this by omitting the clause or using another phrase that does not have this clause as some unmerciful men try to do (as Chrysostom says). No, by this trickery, whereby they try to deceive God himself, they merit greater wrath. This sentence of God remains pure: "If you do not forgive men their sins, your Father will not forgive your sins" (Matt. 6:15).

In the Chaldean language, "debtors" means those who have offended us, who have done something against us, or, as Paul says, "whatever grievances you may have against one another" (Col. 3:13). Luke adds, "We forgive every man that is indebted to us." By nature we desire to be kinder and gentler to some and harder toward others. By nature we bear those injuries and wrongs that are done to us by great men with less sorrow and grief than those that are done to us by our peers or inferiors.

Therefore, he takes away all prejudice in this brotherly forgiving when he says, "We forgive every one who is indebted to us." Here he speaks not properly and principally of civil debts. Civil debt is to be forgiven or at least tolerated if it cannot be repaid without the loss and hurt of our neighbor. The parable in Matthew 18:33 plainly teaches us this. Therefore, Augustine properly advises us to be repulsed more by the hatred of our brother than by other sins. He says, "that those things by which you have offended others through your wants and needs might here be cured when you say, 'Forgive us our debts.' Your stubborn hatred and desire for revenge will spoil you since 'even as we forgive others' is added. Being spoiled, all your sins are retained and nothing forgiven."[2]

Now he who did the wrong and he who is wronged both are commanded to be reconciled. "If you are offering your gift at the altar and there remember that your brother has something against you," that is, has any quarrel against you because you wronged him, "first go and be reconciled to your brother" (Matt. 5:23–24). Without reconciliation you cannot deal with God or ask forgiveness. He who has wrong done to him is commanded, "if he sins against you seven times in a day, and seven times comes back to you and says, 'I repent,' forgive him"; yes, not seven times but seventy-seven times (Luke 17:4). "Whatever you loose on earth will be loosed in heaven" (Matt. 18:18). But if your brother who has offended you does not repent, though you forgive him, God in heaven does not forgive him, seeing that he does not repent. Christ here speaks of public reconciliation (Luke 17:3). His meaning is not that we may or ought keep and exercise our anger, hatred, and bitterness. Our anger must not cause us to not forgive our adversary when he repents and asks forgiveness. The commandment is general. "And when you stand praying, if you hold anything against anyone, forgive him, so that your Father in heaven may forgive you your sins" (Mark 11:25). Therefore, in our heart we forgive our debtors privately, even when they do not repent or ask us for forgiveness.

This brotherly forgiveness has many points. We should not conceive anger or hatred against our neighbor who

2. Reference unknown.

wronged us unjustly. We should lay aside and put away anger, hatred, and enmity conceived against our neighbor for wrong done to us. We should neither take revenge, think upon, nor endeavor to take revenge upon our neighbor. No, we should not covet or desire that either God himself or any other person should give temporal or eternal punishment on him for wrong done to us. Only when the Order of Justice commands it can this happen. We must rather wish for them the godly desire to correct their wrong, that being converted they may be saved eternally and not be condemned. If they have not repented, we must desire that they may in time be chastened and corrected. So that they may be spared eternally, we ask that God's pity and compassion will give fatherly scourges of bit and bridle. Thus we ought to love our enemies, wishing and praying for all things that bring them to salvation. Also, we ought to pray for those who persecute us so, that even this sin may not be charged to them.

Chapter 10

"AND LEAD US NOT INTO TEMPTATION"

There are various kinds of temptations. God is said to tempt[1] but only for good. Sometimes he sends us some peril, some adversity, or postpones help and deliverance. By this he tries and exercises us. He proves our satisfaction, faith, hope, patience, obedience, and constancy. But temptation to do or desire evil comes either from the devil, the flesh, or the world. The devil properly is called the Tempter (1 Thess. 3:5), "the tempter might have tempted you" means that he goes about to draw us from that which is good or to seduce us into evil. He does this either by inward suggestion or else by some outward occasion of prosperity or adversity. He tempts us on the right hand or on the left. The flesh tempts us

---

1. A helpful discussion between the meanings of "tempt" is found in *Luther's Small Catechism with Explanation*: "228. What do *tempt* and *temptation* mean in the Scriptures? In the Scriptures these words have two meanings: A. The testing of our faith, which God uses to bring us closer to himself [Here the Catechism cites John 6:5–6 and James 1:2–3] … B. The attempts of our spiritual enemies to lure us away from God and his ways [Here the Catechism cites Mark 14:38 and James 1:13–14]" (St. Louis: Concordia, 1991, p. 191).

into evil when we are tempted and drawn away by our own evil concupiscence. Concupiscence is the inborn inclination to sin. This lust conceives sin and sin brings forth death. The world tempts either by evil examples, as it were, by laying stumbling blocks and offenses in front of us, or else by exerting actual evil pressures. Ancient writers say that the world flatters so that it may deceive. It terrifies us so that it may confound us. Every such temptation comes by either positive or negative situations. It can come by pleasant, delectable things appealing to our covetous nature, evil desire, and wicked love. It can also come by those things that are sorrowful and fearful, or by those things that inspire great fear, dread, and the need to escape. To explain the meaning of this petition, the distinction of Gregory is very good. He says, "temptation is caused by suggestion, by delight, and by consent."

The distinction of some ancient writers is very good for consideration. They say that the devil uses the following wiles, crafts, and deceits to tempt and upset those who are wise and strong: 1) when affliction lasts long and deliverance is slow in coming; 2) when the misery seems too very great, very peculiar, and very strange; 3) when under the goal of doing some great good, he challenges some to try something very dangerous or something beyond their strength and vocation; 4) when he cloaks and covers evil under the name of virtue, such as coveting being called guidance, cruelty called justice, pride called bravery, ignorance called simplicity, waste called liberality, and so forth; and 5) when he uses peace, quietness, and rest to tempt into a feeling of false security.

Now we are not commanded to pray that God would not try us by his temptations. We receive good from God in tribulation, for we know that affliction brings forth patience, and patience trial, and trial hope (Rom. 5:4). "Consider it pure joy, my brothers, whenever you face trials of many kinds" (James 1:2). Neither do we pray that we may completely be freed from the darts of Satan, of the flesh, or of the world. "He that is not tempted, what does he know?" questions the son of Sirach (Ecclesiasticus 34:10). Augustine, concerning the sixtieth Psalm, says, "By temptation comes our increase. For no man knows himself unless he is tempted. No man can be king unless he wins and no man wins unless he fights. Neither can he fight unless he has enemies who challenge him."[2] In the fourteenth book of *The City of God* he says, "if we have no temptation or troubles at all while we bear the frailty of this life, we do not live properly."[3] This may be the proper understanding of the prayer of Christ in John 17:15. He says, "My prayer is not that you take them out of the world but that you protect them from evil."[4]

The words of this petition do not mean "that we may not be tempted," but "that we may not be led into temptation." Bernard cites Cyprian,[5] who says that it is one thing to be tempted or assaulted with temptation and another thing to be led into temptation. It is one thing when we are openly tempted and have to struggle with it. It is another thing when being tempted, oppressed, and overwhelmed by it, that we fall down under it and are overcome, either consenting to it or completely giving in to it. To be led into temptation is to be tantalized with the idea of some sin, to be carried totally into it, and to completely consent to the temptation. Christ uses a word that means not so much to "lead into" as to "carry into." Augustine also commented on this when anything is said to be "led" or "carried into." When the Greek interpreters trans-

---

2. Augustine, "Psalm Sixty-One," paragraph 2.

3. Augustine, *The City of God*, trans. Marcus Dodds, D. D., II (New York: Hofner Publishing, 1948), p. 18.

4. At this place the NIV is modified to reflect Chemnitz' understanding of the Greek of John 17. His presentation centers on the difference between the neuter and masculine gender of the Greek word for evil. For Chemnitz when this word is used in the neuter it is to be translated evil, but when used in the masculine it is to be translated evil one. Since this is a work by Chemnitz, his understanding as to translation will take precedence over the editors of the NIV.

5. Cyprian, "On the Lord's Prayer," Treatise IV, paragraph 26, p. 56

lated from the Hebrew, they used the verb that means "to bring to," "to bring upon," "to lead into," "to carry into." The Hebrew word is used in the same sense about the worshipping of the calf. "You led them into such great sin" (Ex. 32:21). "You would have brought guilt upon us" (Gen. 26:10). "I... would bring down curse on myself rather than a blessing" (Gen. 27:12). "You brought us into..." (Ps. 66:11). "I will not bring this disaster in his day" (1 Kings 21:29).

The understanding of the phrase "to lead or carry into temptation" is central to understanding the meaning of this petition. It may best be understood by studying its use. The Scripture speaks of the assault or sending of temptation, saying, "No temptation has seized you except what is common to man" (1 Cor. 10:13). Scripture says to "Consider it pure joy... whenever you face trials of many kinds" (James 1:2). This does not merely mean to fall into temptation but rather to run into, to bite upon temptation. What Paul says is more serious. He says that men fall into temptation as if it were a snare, "fall into temptation... and many foolish and harmful desires that plunge men into ruin and destruction" (1 Tim. 6:9). "Pray that you will not fall into temptation" (Luke 22:40), lest unknowingly, worrying about armor or battle plans, you are surrounded by temptation that may overcome you, may even drown you. From this it is clear that we are led into temptation when we are left to ourselves, destitute of the help of God. Then we are driven, plunged, thrust down, or cast head first into the skills and mighty assaults of the devil's temptations. We are bound to be overwhelmed by them as though we were in every way trapped in sin. We do not pray for only one person, that we alone may not be led into temptation. When we are speaking to our heavenly Father, we say, "Lead us not into temptation." Augustine notes that many translate this petition as "suffer us not to be led into temptation," but the meaning is more proper if it is translated as, "lead us not...."

We must remember that we fight not with flesh and blood,

but against the powers of darkness and spiritual deception (Eph. 6:12). Because the deceptiveness of temptation far exceeds our strength (really, our weakness), there is great danger in underestimating its power lest we give in to temptation, are overcome by it, and so drown in perdition. Therefore, first of all we pray asking that Satan not have freedom to tempt us as much as either he would or could. We also ask that he tempt us only as much as God permits and gives permission (Job 1:12). We pray that our heavenly Father would not cast us off and deliver us to the lust, to the treasons, and to the power of this Tempter. We pray that he would remove and temper the temptation and not allow us to be tempted past that which by his grace and gift we are able to bear (1 Cor. 10:13).

Second, when Satan desires to tempt us or to winnow us, we pray that our heavenly Father would not forsake us and leave us by ourselves. We pray that he would not deprive us of his ever-present grace and help in the time of temptation. We ask that he would be present with us and assist us to drive away, to repel, to suppress, and to bridle the devil. We ask that he would be present, ministering strength and courage to us. Being strong in the Lord and in the power of his might (Eph. 6:13), we ask to be able to bear the temptation (James 1:12), withstand it (1 Pet. 5:10), and not yield or be overcome by it. We ask for strength so as not to faint in the time of temptation (Luke 8:13) or be overwhelmed in perdition (1 Tim. 6:9). But we ask that, repelling them all, we may be able to fight and stand fast (Eph. 6:11). We ask that in the time of temptation we may be kept from evil (John 17:15). We also ask that Christ our Mediator (Luke 22:32) pray for us, that our faith, hope, patience, struggling, and constancy may not fail.

Third, we think ourselves to be secure, rather than acknowledging that we are unprepared and drowsy in time of temptation. We do not consider the arrows and power of this Tempter or our own many weaknesses. Neither are we very careful about the danger of temptation. Therefore, we must pray that the Lord himself would awaken us out of the sleep of security as he teaches his Apostles (Luke 22:46). We pray that we may watch, praying with all boldness and fervor so that we are not led into temptation. Also we pray that God himself would arm us, giving us wisdom and strength so that we may well use his weapons to oppose temptations.

Fourth, we pray that God would give us patience, consolation, and hope (Rom. 5:4). No matter how long or how seriously God will have us be tempted, we ask that we may be able to bear it, being content with the grace of God just like Paul (2 Cor. 12:9).

Fifth, we pray that, when we are trapped by temptation and cannot free ourselves or find any way out, he would give such a gift[6] that we may be able to sustain and bear it. We ask that this may even be profitable for us and result in the glory of God (1 Cor. 10:13).

Sixth, because he knows that we have so little strength, we pray that Christ would keep us from the dangerous and deadly hour of temptation (Rev. 3:3).

Seventh, in the time of temptation, we ask God that he would keep us from the pride of Peter and the despair of Saul [Paul]!

Eighth, we pray that God in his wrath would not punish one sin with another and so lead us into worse temptation, as he did David (2 Sam. 24:1; 1 Chron. 21:1). We ask that he would not give us up to the lust of our own hearts (Ps. 81:12) or into a reprobate mind (Rom. 1:28). We ask him not to give us hardness of heart so that we should not grieve for our sins (Eph. 4:18). This interpretation, being taken out of the Scripture itself, is the most simple and proper one.

These things we must pray for in general for the whole Church, privately for ourselves, and by name for others who

---

6. The 1598 text has "an issue."

are being tempted. We desire deliverance from evils, bless-ings, and a spirit of thanksgiving for those benefits we receive. We confess that we do not strongly strive against temptations. We give into them, do not prepare ourselves in the face of temptations, and do not put on the armor of God. We confess that we ourselves set up opportunity for the Tempter when we sweep and dress up the house (Luke 11:25) and offer our own bodies as weapons to the Tempter (Rom. 6:19). All this we have explained before and here only briefly point out the chief teachings. Later we will fully meditate upon this petition.

Now this petition contains a general confession for the weakness and infirmity in this life in the whole Church, that is the children of God. When we pray that we may not give in to temptation nor be overcome by it, we acknowledge and confess that by our own strength we are not able to resist any temptations. We acknowledge that this is the work of God's grace. We acknowledge that after we have received new spir-itual strength through our rebirth, God's grace and strength directly follow.

Chapter 11

"BUT DELIVER US FROM EVIL"

Some would not have this petition stand by itself. The adversative conjunction[1] "but," which is used here, can be used with the force of joining two clauses into one thought. If this were so, we would be praying in the negative, "lead us not," and positively praying for the same things here by saying "deliver us." I would not argue with anyone about this matter. Yet I think the doctrine of the Catechism in order to better instruct simply calls this the seventh petition. It is larger and contains more in it than the sixth petition contains concerning temptation. Rather than fruitlessly arguing, I will simply begin the explanation.

The word in the common Greek tongue translated as "deliver" signifies the two following things. First, it means to defend, to protect, to keep, and to preserve from evil that we fall not into it. Homer uses it in *Iliad 10*,[2] where it is connected

---

1. The 1598 text has "particle."
2. Homer, *The Iliad of Homer*, trans. William Cullen Bryant (Boston: Houghton Mifflin, 1898), p. 259.

with a word that signifies "to keep"; and in *Iliad 15*,[3] he uses it in the phrase "which before defends you." Second, it means to take and deliver out of the evil in which we are now. We pray to be kept and to be delivered from evil. The Greek interpreters translated those Hebrew words that mean "to pluck away" and "to deliver out of the enemies' hand" with this same word. It is used this way for the most part in the New Testament. But 1 Thessalonians 1:10 seems to contain both these meanings as it is applied to Jesus, "who rescues us from the coming wrath." In Romans 5:9, instead of the term "to save" it says: "how much more shall we be saved from God's wrath." Christ, referring to this petition, uses the word "protect." "My prayer is not that you take them out of the world but that you protect them from the evil one" (John 17:15). Therefore it is proper to understand it in both ways, to be kept from and to be delivered from evil.

Chrysostom takes the words as masculine and explains it as the devil himself. The devil is not only evil himself but is the author and mediator of all evil when it is hurtful and deadly for us. He is our enemy, seeking to devour us, and like a spiteful person he rejoices at our evil. In the New Testament Satan is referred to as the "evil one" when it is used in the masculine without a substantive article. The neuter gender of this word is rarely used by itself in the New Testament. It is used most often with a substantive article like evil men, evil hearts, evil works, or evil thoughts. Yet the Greek interpreters translated the same word as an evil thing. They understand it either as sin (Gen. 39:9, where it denotes adultery with his master's wife), hindrance, danger, loss, or adversity (1 Sam. 25:18, where it denotes giving evil for good, just like in the New Testament). In this petition, therefore, we understand evil of itself in the masculine for the devil himself. In the neuter we

---

3. *Ibid.*, p. 72.

understand it as sin and as any hurt, danger, or adversity that burdens the soul, body, possessions, or good name. It includes things now here or what hangs over our head.

First, therefore, seeing that the devil walks about like a roaring lion seeking whom he may devour, we pray that God would mercifully defend, preserve, keep, save, and protect us from him and from all his skills, snares, temptations, and cruelty. If the devil has entangled and caught us in his snares and temptations, we pray that God would pluck us from them and deliver us.

Second, we pray that God would keep us from every sin or evil work so that we fall into no sin.

Third, we pray that he would keep, protect, and defend us from the sorrows of the life to come, that is, from everlasting pain. We also ask that he would defend us from all dangers, losses, hindrances, and adversities of this life as relating to our soul and body, our possessions, and good name. We ask that he would stop, repel, and turn back these things since they are evil. If we are already burdened with these evils, we pray that in his mercy he would free and deliver us from them. When using the word "evil" we include all that God knows, perceives, or judges to be not good and wholesome for us but rather dangerous and deadly.

Fourth, we desire many things to be given us which we consider good and proper for us. We also want to be preserved and delivered from many things, things that we scarcely know whether they would be profitable unto us or not. Because of these we add in the conclusion of this prayer that if we ask anything that he knows and perceives would not be good, but rather hurtful for us, that he would keep and deliver us from evil.

Fifth, if God sees that it is not good and profitable for us, he should take from us the messenger of Satan who taunts us. He should keep and deliver us from adversity. We pray that he would give us patience, obedience, consolation, and hope so that we may acknowledge his fatherly care over us. We acknowledge this so that those things that God sends us for our good might not become hurtful to us. In the past they used to pray in adversity using very good and godly brevity. They would pray, "God either deliver them, stop their misery, or preserve them by giving them patience."

Sixth, this protection and deliverance from evil in this life are not complete and perfect. These are only accomplished in part, for daily there arise new assaults by the devil, by sin, and by enemies. These three assaults are always around us, therefore we pray that eventually we may be perfectly and completely delivered and set free. Because such deliverance cannot happen to us in this world or in this life, for it is warfare and as the Greeks translated it, "the rousing of a pirate," we are actually asking for eternal life in this petition. We believe, as stated in the Creed, that we may be taken out of this world where the devil is prince and given everlasting life. We desire to leave the earth, this vale of tears that brings forth thorns and thistles of sorrow, and be taken into another world of eternal life where we shall be free and safe from all evils. We ask that we may not always be subject and exposed to the darts, temptations, and assaults of the devil, the world, the flesh, and tragedy. Paul says in Romans 7:24, "What a wretched man I am! Who will rescue me from this body of death?" He demonstrates a godly and excellent feeling when he says,

> At my first defense, no one came to my support… but the Lord stood at my side and gave me strength… and I was delivered from the lion's mouth. The Lord will rescue me from every evil attack and will bring me safely to his heavenly kingdom. To him be glory for ever and ever. Amen. (2 Tim. 4:16–18)

In these words he really is repeating the last petition and conclusion of the Lord's Prayer.

Seventh, we are taught in the petition to lift up our heads, to think upon, and to desire the blessed life to come. This life is eternal where there will be full deliverance from all evil. Because we are too occupied and immersed in the matters and affairs of this world and of this life, we also request that God would inspire, excite, kindle, generate, and preserve in us this thought and desire. We earnestly desire release from this world, that is, to leave this life and to enter blessed life. Every kind of death is not the end of misery, for the death of the wicked is just the beginning of their torments (Luke 16:22). The death of the godly is their deliverance from all evil and a beginning of everlasting happiness.

Therefore, when we say, "Deliver us from evil," we desire that our heavenly Father would keep us from an evil death. We ask for his deliverance so that we may not "die the death of the uncircumcised" (Ezek. 28:10) or the death of sinners. This would be the worst of all (Ps. 34:22). We ask that we may not die carelessly in our sins, unprepared without repentance (John 8:24), but that he would grant us a godly and saving end of this life. We ask to die in the Lord (Rev. 14:13). We know that whether we live or die, we are the Lord's (Rom. 14:8). Whether we abide as a pilgrim in this life or are called home to our own country by death, we desire to please the Lord (2 Cor. 5:9).

Furthermore, we pray that God would put into us a concern and desire to prepare ourselves in advance for those things that are necessary to be properly prepared for death. This is done so that we may be prepared for death, because we do not want to be like those who do not have oil in their lamps when the bridegroom comes and calls us (Matt. 25:3). We ask that in the last hour of this life we may have true repentance, the Word, the Sacraments, faith, hope, and the spirit of grace and prayer. These things we ask so that when we are to die, we may be found in Christ, having that righteousness that is of God through faith in Christ. In this we rightly commend our souls into the hands of our Father. If we are found improperly prepared, we pray that he would not allow this to happen by a sudden unannounced death, but would mercifully grant us time for such preparation. We ask that our death may be a deliverance from all evil and a passage out of this vale of misery to eternal life. In this petition we ask the Lord mercifully to be present with us in that last and dangerous conflict. By his presence we may ask to be kept and delivered from all evil because our adversary goes about most busily, marking whether he can snatch us away and devour us. We ask that he would strengthen us that we may not fear to die, nor be afraid of death. We ask that when we taste death we may depart in peace and be truly delivered from all evil.

These things we must pray for in this petition, both generally and in particular, desiring blessings from the Lord, praying against evils, giving thanks for benefits received, and confessing our own sins.

Chapter 12

"FOR THINE IS THE KINGDOM..."

The Latin copies do not have this clause, in agreement with it not being in Saint Luke, and neither have Latin writers explained it (see Cyprian,[1] Ambrose,[2] Jerome[3] and Augustine). All Greek copies consistently have it. The Syrian interpreters translated it and Chrysostom also treats it. Likewise in 2 Timothy 4:17, recalling the last petition, "deliver us from evil," Paul adds this clause, "to whom be glory forever and ever." This clause does very properly conclude the whole prayer. It especially reminds God of his promise and, as it were, of his office. It shows the reason we ask these things of God and hope that he will give them to us.

"For Thine is the kingdom" is not understood as God's universal kingdom over all creatures. It is understood of that kingdom which is called the kingdom of heaven, the king-

---

1. Cyprian, "On the Lord's Prayer," Treatise IV, paragraph 29f.

2. Ambrose, "De Sacramentis," *Patrologiae Cursus Completus Patrologiae Latinae*, accurante J. P. Migne, XVI (Paris: Apud Garnier Fratres, 1880), p. 473.

3. Jerome, "Against Jovinians," Book 2, paragraph 3; also "Against the Pelagians," Book 3, paragraph 15.

dom of God, and of Christ in the Church. These things that we ask are the blessings of that kingdom. God has set up his kingdom for our need against the devil, the world, and the flesh. For as much as we cannot create these things for which we ask from ourselves, neither can we achieve them by ourselves, we ask that we might receive them from his hand in his own kingdom. It belongs to the office of our King in this kingdom, that he should keep and defend us against the devil, the world, and the flesh. It is he who should give to those who believe and who pray for these blessings. He has commanded us to ask and has promised to grant our requests.

By these words this prayer reminds God to be mindful of his own commandment, of his promise, and of his office in his kingdom. In all this, these words show the reason why one asks these things and seeks for them not from any other, but from God alone.

These words, "Thine is the power," teach us that God has these things that we ask in his hand and in his power. Although the power of the world and of the devil is great, only God can give these things to us perfectly and beneficially. Therefore, we desire these things of him alone.

By the word "glory," faith presents to God that which is a glorious thing to him. If he shall hear us and shall grant us those things that we ask according to his commandment and promise as citizens of his kingdom, this shall greatly bring about the glory, praise, fame of his mercy, his power, and his bountifulness. In this clause we pray that God for Christ's sake, whose kingdom properly this is, by his grace would hear us and grant our requests for the display of the bounty and glory and power of this kingdom.

Second, this clause also serves to stir up and to confirm the faith of those who pray confidently that they shall be heard. For since it says, "Thine is the kingdom," benefits must be given. It is his will to give such benefits. We always are to remember that he has commanded us to ask in his kingdom and has promised to hear us. In these words faith demonstrates the certainty of God's good will toward us. With all its might faith professes in prayer that it relies not on any merit or worthiness of its own, but alone on the favor of God for Christ's sake. For this kingdom is the kingdom of Christ and of grace. Then he attaches power to the will of God, for he says, "Thine is the power." Being assured that God is both willing and able to perform those things that we ask, faith, therefore, neither can nor ought doubt that God hears us. Because we say, "Thine is the glory," faith acknowledges that being faithful in performing the glory of his truth, of his grace, and of his power, God will surely accomplish those things that we ask, lest the heathen say, "Where is now their God?"

Third, the clause "For Thine is the Kingdom" shows us how we are to use those benefits that we desire in prayer. It also shows us for what goal we are to ask. It reminds us where we are to refer them and to what goal we here promise to seek. It shows us what thankfulness we here promise God. As it is said in Psalm 145:11, "They will tell of the glory of your kingdom and speak of your might, so that all men may know of your mighty acts and the glorious splendor of your kingdom." Now as to what is the glory of God's kingdom and as to how it is to be made great, the whole psalm teaches from beginning to end. So this clause or conclusion of the Lord's Prayer teaches us very many things.

Chapter 13

"AMEN"

T his is a Hebrew word, derived from a verb that signifies to believe and to trust, from which also comes the words for faith and truth in the Hebrew tongue. It is very significant and therefore is used in other tongues. Because in the word "amen" the nature of justifying faith in applying its promise to prayer is loudly proclaimed, we must diligently show what it means. So that I may explain it better, I will give very precise examples of its use. The word "amen" is especially used in the following ways:

First, in cursing, Deuteronomy 27:15–16 says, "Cursed is the man… then all the people shall say, 'Amen.'" Numbers 5:20–22 says, "If… you have not gone astray… but if you have gone astray, may the LORD cause your people to curse… Then the woman is to say, 'Amen, so be it.' " Rabbi David says that the word "amen" was spoken as a way of prayer or as a way of asserting that if they themselves had sinned, they took to themselves and upon themselves those curses.

Second, "amen" is used for the most part in prayer or invocation, in blessing and thanksgiving. When prayers and thanksgivings are rehearsed, the Church answers, "Amen" (1 Cor. 14:16) or "Amen, amen" (Ps. 41:13). In Nehemiah 8:6, "Ezra blessed the LORD, the great God; and all the people lifted up their hands and responded, 'Amen! Amen!'" They all say, "Amen" at the marriage blessing (Tob. 12:9). They worshipped God saying, "Amen. Praise and glory and wisdom and thanks and honor and power and strength be to our God for ever and ever. Amen!" (Rev. 7:12). It is not a mere wishing and desiring. By faith it is a true desire of the heart that asks and by true hope expects that those things for which we ask in prayer will be done and accomplished. In the *Story of Samosatenus* by Eusebius and in the *Fourth Book of the Sacraments* by Ambrose,[1] when in the administration of the Lord's Supper, the bread of the Lord is given to everyone with these words, "Take, eat, this is the body of Christ given for you for the remission of sins," we find then every communicant answered "Amen."

There is a usage of the word "amen" worth noting in 1 Kings 1:36. When David had commanded that Solomon should be anointed king to succeed him, he commanded them to say, "God save King Solomon." Benias answered and said, "Amen. The Lord, God of my lord the king, says so, too."

Muntzer[2] says that it is the imperative passive of the first conjugation of the word *Heaman*. Therefore, the meaning of it should be this: "Let this be true, let this be ratified and confirmed of the Lord." The Chaldean dictionary says it is the future tense, having the first letter removed, *Ieamen*, meaning "let this be confirmed or established." The Greeks, regarding the root, have usually translated 1 Kings 1:36 as "so be it, the Lord God ratify and do the word of my lord the king."

---

1. Ambrose, "De Sacramentis," *Patrologiae Cursus Completus Patrologiae Latinae*, accurante J. P. Migne, XVI (Paris: Apud Garnier Fratres, 1880), p. 463

2. Possibly Muntzer, *Hebraicae Grammaticae* (Basel: [n.n.], 1536).

Third, the word "amen" is also used when faith receives a promise offered. In 1 Chronicles 16:36, after the listing of the promises of God, this is added: "Then all the people said 'Amen.' " In Jeremiah 11:4–5, the Lord repeats this promise: " 'I will be your God. Then I will fulfill the oath I swore to your forefathers…' I answered, 'Amen, Lord.' " In Jeremiah 28:6, when Hananiah prophesied of the coming prosperity, Jeremiah says, "Amen." Jeremiah here adds a large exposition of the word "amen." He says, "May the LORD do so; may the LORD fulfill the words you have prophesied." Mary has famously expressed the meaning of this word. She says "May it be to me as you have said" (Luke 1:38). These two meanings are almost identical. Yet for plainness' sake I thought it good to distinguish between the fact that the properties of faith in applying the promise and of faith in praying might be better understood by the use of the word "amen."

Fourth, "amen" is used for a note of affirmation and solemn declaration. The promises of God are not "yes" and "no" (as though in them one thing might be said in words and another thing thought in the heart, or else might be promised in words and in deed not be done), "They are 'yes' in Christ. And so through him the 'amen' is spoken by us" (2 Cor. 1:20). Here the Hebrew word "amen" is translated by the Greek word "yes." This "yes" is a sign of affirming and declaring. "Whoever invokes a blessing in the land will do so by the God of truth; he who takes an oath in the land will do so by the God of truth" (Is. 65:16). Whereas the Greek word "yes" is a sign of swearing when anything is affirmed and vowed as though an oath were to it, just so is the word "amen." This last understanding agrees with those places in the Gospels where Christ says, "Amen, I say unto you." The root word and all the words derived from it mean truth, certainty, stability, and constancy. When it is referred to someone speaking, its meaning is this: I speak not at random, rashly, or lightly, but truly, certainly, earnestly, and constantly. It is "I say, I affirm and vow as if I had sworn." If it refers to that which is spoken, it has this sense: that which I say is no wavering thought or doubtful opinion, but it is true, certain, sure, and stable. It is neither changed nor altered but is undoubtedly so decreed in the will of God and shall indeed be so accomplished. The doubling of the word "amen, amen" enforces the declaration and may well be understood as a superlative which the Hebrew language does not have. An example might be "What I say is most sure and firm."

Furthermore, the word "amen" in the Septuagint is sometimes expressed by the verb "so be it" (Deut. 27:15, 26; Ps. 41:13; 1 Kings 1:36; Numb. 5:22). Sometimes it is translated by the word "truly" (Jer. 28:6). Sometimes the Hebrew word is still used, as in 1 Chronicles 16:36, "Then all the people said 'Amen'" (Jer. 11:5, Neh. 8:6, Tob. 8:9). The word "amen" is used in the Greek tongue and is retained in the New Testament. When Mark refers to the widow in verse 12:43, he says, "Amen, I say to you."[3] In Luke 21:3, Luke recounts it as, "Amen, I say to you."[4]

Since this prayer is concluded with the word[5] "amen," it teaches us that when we come to the end of our prayer we must consider with what devotion we have prayed. We must ask if we have been mumbling words coldly. After we expressed our needs and requests and after praying, our mind is excited and stirred up so that we bring forth an earnest request from the

---

3. The normal NIV is not used. The simple translation of the Greek is used in the 1598 Edition and is used here since the word "Amen" is actually in the Greek but translated differently in the NIV.

4. Although the NIV reflects the accepted Greek text using the word "truly," the 1598 Edition uses the work "Amen". The arguments of Chemnitz in this particular paragraph requires the abandonment of the NIV for the rendition Chemnitz uses. The reader must remember that the critical editions of the Greek text were not available to Chemnitz.

5 The 1598 text has "particle."

very heart; then the heat of our desires is kindled and flames up brightly. Humbly and devoutly, our inward sighs wish and desire that our prayer may be ratified and confirmed by God. It is our desire that our heavenly Father, for Christ our Mediator's sake, would bow down his ear, hear and receive our prayer, and do those things which we desire. "Amen, amen" means "let it be done, let it be done, O Lord, that which I have asked."

By this word "amen," faith shows itself not to doubt or to be carried about with the waves of mistrust. Faith does not doubt whether God will hear us and will do those things for which we ask. Instead, it strongly confesses that as God has commanded us to ask and has promised that he will hear, so he will faithfully perform and accomplish our requests. Again, by this word, faith stirs up itself, upholds, defends, and confirms itself against doubting. For it takes the word "amen" from that promise "I tell you the truth… I will do whatever you ask in my name." Here he joins his own "amen" as if it were a seal. Here he makes a great confession that God is faithful and true (John 14:12–13). Jerome very finely calls this word "amen" the "seal of prayer."

INDEX

INDEX OF NAMES

SCRIPTURAL INDEX

TOPICAL INDEX

SELECTED BIBLIOGRAPHY

A Complete Listing of Works by Chemnitz

Mahlmann, Theodor, "Bibliographie Martin Chemnitz" in *Der zweite Martin der Lutherische Kirke*, ed. Wolfgang A. Jünke (Braunschweig: Ev.–luth. Stadtkirkenverband und Propstei Braunschweig, 1986).

Rehtmeyer, Philippo Julio, *Antiqvitates Ecclestiaticae inclytae urbiz Braunsvigae, oder: Der Beruhmten Stadt Braunschweig Kirchenhistorie* Braunschweig: Gedruckt Verlagt von Christoph Friedrich Zilligers, 1710).

Williams, D. Georg, "The Works of Martin Chemnitz," *Concordia Theological Quarterly*, XLII, 1978.

Chemnitz' Works in English

"An Autobiography of Martin Chemnitz," trans. A. L. Graebner. *Theological Quarterly*, 3:4 (1899).

Examination of the Council of Trent, vols. 1–4, trans. Fred Kramer (St. Louis: Concordia, 1971–1986).

"Free Will" and "Sin," *The Doctrine of Man in Classical Lutheran Theology* ed. H. A. Press and Edmund Smits (Minneapolis: Augsburg, 1962).

Justification: The Chief Article of Christian Doctrine as Expounded in Loci Theologici, trans. J. A. O. Preus (St. Louis: Concordia, 1985).

Loci Theologici, vols. 1 and 2, trans. J. A. O. Preus (St. Louis: Concordia, 1989).

The Lord's Supper, trans. J. A. O. Preus (St. Louis: Concordia, 1979).

Ministry, Word, and Sacraments: An Enchiridion, trans. Luther Poellot (St. Louis: Concordia, 1981).

The Two Natures in Christ, trans. J. A. O. Preus (St. Louis: Concordia, 1971).

Works about Chemnitz in English

Cooper, W. H. "Martin Chemnitz on Justification: With Special Reference to His Use of the Old Testament," *Northwestern Seminary Bulletin*, XXX (1960).

Elert, Werner, *The Structure of Lutheranism*, trans. Walter A. Hansen (St. Louis: Concordia, 1962).

Fagerberg, Holsten, *A New Look at the Lutheran Confessions*, trans. Gene J. Lunt, (St. Louis: Concordia, 1972).

Green, Lowell C., "The Three Causes of Conversion in Philipp Melanchthon, Martin Chemnitz, David Chytraeus, and the 'Formula of Concord,' " *Lutherjahrbuch*, 47 (1980).

Jacobs, Henry Eyster, "Chemnicius Redivivus," *The Evangelical Quarterly Review*, XXI (1870).

_____, "Martin Chemnitz and the Council of Trent," *The Evangelical Quarterly Review*, XXI (1870).

Jungkuntz, Theodore R., *Formulators of the Formula of Concord* (St. Louis: Concordia, 1977).

Klug, E. F., "Chemnitz on Trent—An Unanswered Challenge," *Christianity Today*, 17:23 (1973).

_____, *From Luther to Chemnitz: On Scripture and the Word* (Grand Rapids: William B. Eerdmans, 1971).

_____, "Luther and Chemnitz on Scripture," *Springfielder*, 37:3 (1973).

Kolb, Robert, "Dynamics of Party Conflict in Saxon Late Reformation: Gnesio-Lutherans vs. Philippists," *The Journal of Modern History Supplement*, 49:3 (1977).

Kramer, Fred, "Martin Chemnitz," *Shapers of Tradition in Germany, Switzerland, and Poland, 1560–1600*, ed. Jill Rait (New Haven: Yale University Press, 1981).

_____, "Martin Chemnitz on the Authority of the Sacred Scriptures: An Examination of the Council of Trent," *Springfielder*, 37:3 (1973).

Kriewaldt, E., "The Life and Work of Martin Chemnitz," *The Australasion Theological Review*, 7:2 (1936).

Neitzel, Elmer August, "Shades of Martin Chemnitz," *Springfielder*, 37:3 (1973).

Olson, A. L., "Martin Chemnitz and the Council of Trent," *dialog*, II (1963).

_____, *Scripture and Tradition in the Theology of Martin Chemnitz* (Cambridge: Harvard University, 1965).

Petersen, Wilhelm, et al., "1985 Bethany Lutheran College Reformation Lectures," *The Lutheran Synod Quarterly*, 25:4 (1985) [Wilhelm Petersen, "A Biographical Sketch of the Life of Martin Chemnitz 1522–1586"; Eugene F. Klug, "Chemnitz and Authority"; J. A. O. Preus, "Martin Chemnitz on the Doctrine of Justification"].

Piepkorn, Arthur Carl, "Martin Chemnitz' Views on Trent: The Genesis and the Genius of the Examen Concilii Tridentini," *Concordia Theological Monthly*, 37:1 (1966).

_____, "The Two Natures in Christ by Martin Chemnitz in English Translation: A Review Article," *Concordia Theological Monthly*, 44:3 (1973).

Preus, J. A. O., "Chemnitz and the Book of Concord," *Concordia Theological Quarterly*, 44:1 (1980).

_____, "Chemnitz on Law and Gospel," *Concordia Journal*, 15 (1989).

_____, *The Second Martin: the Life and Theology of Martin Chemnitz* (St. Louis: Concordia, 1994).

Preus, Robert D., *Getting into the Theology of Concord: A Study of the Book of Concord* (St. Louis: Concordia, 1977).

_____, *The Theology of Post Reformation Lutheranism*, vol. 1–2 (St. Louis: Concordia, 1970–1972).

Preus, Robert D. and Wilbert Rosin, eds., *A Contemporary Look at the Formula of Concord* (St. Louis: Concordia, 1978).

Scaer, David P., *Getting into the Story of Concord: A History of the Book of Concord* (St. Louis: Concordia, 1977).

Teigen, Bjarne W., *The Lord's Supper in the Theology of Martin Chemnitz* (Brewster, MA: Trinity Lutheran Press, 1986).